The Almarick

An Almanac of Limericks

The Almarick

An Almanac of Limericks

By Phil Dowell

A celebration in limerick form of a noted birth, death, or special event for each day of the calendar

First published in Great Britain by (PED)antics in 2019.

Copyright © Phil Dowell 2019.

The moral right of the author has been asserted.

A CIP catalogue record for this book is available from the British Library.

ISBN 978-1-5272-3649-3

Set in Comic Sans and Calibri and designed by the author.

Cover design, print and binding by Creeds Design and Print, Gore Cross, Bridport DT6 3UX.

Published by (PED)antics, 12 Pine View, Bridport DT6 5AE.

Pedanticsltd@gmail.com

About This Book

Chambers Book of Days was my major source of salivation
The *Penguin Rhyming Dictionary* saved me much perspiration
I give thanks to Edward Lear because
I must - but I do not start *There was*
And, unlike Lear, a third rhyme stretched my imagination

Mixing births and deaths with historical events galore
The second version was compiled in 2004
I have nothing but praise
For *Chambers Book of Days*
Though some of the events I found to be rather obscure

If I should have stolen someone's idea
Or otherwise plagiarised, let's be clear
Please treat my bloomer
With a sense of humour
I seek no gain, except to bring good cheer

Limericks should be humorous, so it's said
I looked for an angle in the stuff I read;
Applied my unique style
To try and make you smile;
If I don't, then may I make you think instead?

If you, dear reader, would like an affirmative
That mine is good, but yours is superlative
Do please contact me
And allow me to see
The verse you claim is a better alternative

A Note About Dates

This is all about The Calendar (New Style) Act
Of 1750 (as a matter of fact)
Folks reckoned that the cost
Was eleven days lost
It could have been explained with a little more tact

The Act set out to bring Britain, which used the Julian Calendar, into line with most of Europe where the Gregorian was preferred. *New style* refers to a Gregorian date, *old style* to a Julian.

In the Julian Calendar by the way
The first day of New Year's fell on Lady Day
The switch to First of Jan
Was part of the plan
To match the Gregorian, so they say

This change was implemented in the year 1751, which began on 25th March and ended on 31st December, a total of 282 days, the shortest ever.

William Willett, with fools in his sights
Wagered he'd dance for twelve days and nights
On the second he got under way
Only to stop the very next day
It was the fourteenth. He claimed his rights

This story is reported in a book about North Staffordshire
by W M Jamieson.

These were the days in September 1752, when Tuesday 2nd was
followed by Wednesday 14th. Tales of riots with people demanding
the return of their 'lost eleven days' are nowadays thought to be an
early urban myth ('cloned' from a Hogarth print). It was the case
nevertheless that if you were born on one of those days, for the rest
of your life there was confusion about your age.

The Calendar Change, intended to align Britain with Europe, became
an issue in the 1754 General Election. Fancy that – Europe featuring
in a General Election!

New Year's Eve

Just take a quiet moment to contemplate
One of the things that makes New Year's Eve so great
As you start to snore
Of this you can be sure
Tomorrow's the best day of the year to date

New Year's Day

New Year's Day has seldom been a red letter
It's hard to see yourself as a go-getter
With so little sleep
But please do not weep
There's an even chance tomorrow will be better

The Next Day

Today is January the second
This is the day when I've always reckoned
A brand new year starts
Melancholy departs
And your lifestyle plans are feeling fecund

An Alternative Scenario

1st January

The native hue of resolution
Is sicklied o'er by your constitution
And the pale cast of thought
Is making you distraught
That your spouse will demand retribution

Referencing Hamlet's suicide speech...

2nd January

You have said you are sorry for New Year's Eve's conclusion
But wound up with an eye socket sporting a contusion
Together with advice
Do not dare do it twice
Or next time you will be in need of a blood transfusion

And now contemplating suicide yourself...

3rd January

Excommunication by the Pope
Is supposed to mean 'abandon hope!'
But it rather did well
For Martin and Fidel
Which suggests that the Pope was a dope

Both *Martin Luther* in 1521 and *Fidel Castro* in 1962 were
excommunicated on this day.

4th January

When he had lived more than one thousand moons
He started to suffer from faints and swoons
With neither a bang nor a whimper
He just became limp, and then limper
And measured out his life in coffee spoons

T S Eliot died in 1965, aged 77. There are 1,001 moons in 77 years.

5th January

In Glastonbury the *Holy Thorn*
Flowered on the day that Christ was born
But when the State
Altered the date
It responded to the change with scorn

The bush that was said to have grown from *Joseph of Aramathea's*
staff would flower regularly on 25th December. When the calendar
changed in 1752, it flowered today (now in 1753), the old style 25th December.
This led to many Feast Days being celebrated on their old style dates.

6th January

This is the day the *Magi* had sight
Of baby Jesus. I think that's right
Regarding Christmastide
Y'know what I am advised?
It *is* the twelfth day, but not the twelfth night

According to Chambers *Book of Days*.

7th January

King Henry was having trouble with the Holy See
So he said 'You know, I think I'm going to break free
And get rid of my spouse
She's no good round the house'
Thus Catherine became the very first divorcee

Catherine of Aragon died on this day in 1536.

8th January

Today sees the birthday of the King
Boy, could that kid from Tupelo sing
When he gyrated his pelvis
It could only be Elvis
The third best singer after Frank and Bing

In 1935.

9th January

Leicester folk say 'Ay up, me duck
'E wore funny, that Peter Cook
I liked 'im 'n Dud
They woz very good
They used to meck me utherarf cluck'

Peter Cook died in 1995. In Leicestershire, no distinction
is made between the sounds 'u' and 'oo'.

10th January

She's famous for her clothes and smells
Much sought after by classy gels
Her financial might
Helped stage Igor's *Rite*
So music's where her legacy tells

Coco Chanel died in 1965. *Igor Stravinsky* was lodging with
her while he composed the highly controversial *Rite of Spring*
for the *Ballets Russes*. Coco guaranteed the production with
an anonymous gift.

11th January

I want you to a-know know
That the *Whisky-a-go-go*
First came to be
In sixty three
It was the first disco-a-co-co

Inevitably, in Los Angeles.

12th January

Hattie W Caraway, I have to confess
Is someone whose celebrity I could not guess
I was pleased when I saw
She came from Arkansas
The very first woman in the US Congress

Elected in 1932, 17 years to the day after Congress refused women the vote.

13th January

Most energetic and tireless
Caruso sang on the wireless
He had *Cav* and *Pag*
Safely in the bag
Great for list'ners who were eyeless

1910 saw (heard?) the first radio broadcast from New York's
Metropolitan Opera. Enrico Caruso starred in *I Pagliacci* and
Cavalleria Rusticana. The first TV broadcast was in 1948.

14th January

They won't let me play a bewitcher
Or anyone trashy (or kitscher)
So I want you to know
Now I'm married to Joe
I can screw my own talking pitcher

Marilyn Monroe married *Joe DiMaggio*, a celebrated
baseball player (though actually a center fielder – but
that's poetic licence for you) on this day in 1954.

15th January

If government gave way to anarchy
Would you be relaxed, or feel panicky?
If a man verbally deft
Said 'Property is theft'
Would you dismiss it as logomachy?

The man quoted, *Pierre Joseph Proudhon*, was born in 1804.
Look up logomachy in a lexicon.

16th January

It was such a ludicrous ruse
When Congress tried to ban all booze
After that, what next?
Hey, how about sex?
Go on – there's no more fun to lose

The 18th Amendment, making the sale of alcohol illegal,
was passed in 1920.

17th January

St Antony's the Patron Saint of pigs
That's not a fact that everybody twigs
He protected the *Tamworth Two*
And when their adventure was through
They retired to luxury *rare breed* digs

On 8th January 1998, two pigs escaped from an abattoir.
Being rare breeds, they attracted media attention and were
dubbed *The Tamworth Two*. They were recaptured after a
week on the run, and on this day their death sentence was
commuted to life in a Rare Breed centre in Kent. We celebrate
St Antony on this day.

18th January

This is the birthday of AA Milne, who
Introduced the world to *Winnie the Pooh*
Throughout the years
Everyone cheers
All apart from *Eeyore*, who just says '*Boo*'

AA Milne was born in 1882.

19th January

Whoever told the tale of Watt and the kettle
Must have been feeling quite smug, and in fine fettle
Like Newton's apple
It helps kids grapple
With a concept which puts them on their mettle

James Watt was born in 1736. He didn't invent the steam engine, and the kettle story is a myth, designed to demonstrate the power of steam pressure.

20th January

Finding land in the ocean's a big deal
So James Cook could have shown a bit more zeal
When he found a land which
He named after a sandwich
As a cook, why not after a hot meal?

Cook named the *Sandwich Islands* (after the Earl) in 1778.

21st January

If you were a Soviet citizen, when in
Moscow, you queued to file past the Tomb of Lenin
Nine million comrades
Gave their accolades
Before the war that they lost that many men in

Lenin was born *Vladimir Ilyich Ulyanov* in 1870.

22nd January

This historical fact is really well known
Victoria was sixty five years on the throne
And then she was gone
In nineteen o one
Was she quite charming, or a bit of a crone?

England's second longest serving monarch died on this day.

23rd January

Django Reinhart is a man one must admire
He played the guitar like *Amphion* played the lyre
When he played with singers
He showed them two fingers
He played with. The rest he damaged in a fire

In Greek mythology Amphion played his lyre, enchanting stones which built themselves into the walls of *Thebes*. *Reinhart* was born in 1910.
He is a famous Belgian.

24th January

Baden Powell was thoroughly cook-a-hoop
When he organised his first Boy Scout troop
If he tried it now
I think somehow
He'd end up in a police station coop

The *Scout Movement* began this day in 1908.

25th January

Great Chieftain of the Pudding Race
Be welcome to this hallowed place
In a moment or two
We'll massacre you
But we're civil, so we'll first say grace

This night is *Burns Night*.

26th January

Today is Australia Day
When every Bruce and Sheila say
'There's a world of wonder
Waiting down under'
If you'll excuse me, I'll stay away

Commemorating the day in 1788 when shiploads of
convicts founded their first colony.

27th January

Think Bach was the best? I say, did he offer us
Forms that a *Classical Composer Proper* does?
For me it was Mozart
With his *tres beaux beaux arts*
Heard in his symphonies, quartets and operas

The world's greatest composer was born this day in 1756.

28th January

Well known for his eccentricity
Walpole first penned 'serendipity'
He was eating posset
When he stumbled across it
Adding to its authenticity

Horace Walpole, son of Sir Robert, coined the word in
a letter to a friend, dated this day in 1754. It refers to
a propensity to make fortunate discoveries unexpectedly.

29th January

There once was a man called Roy Plomley
(Whose name was not spelt as in Cholmondley)
He'd play you a tune
In a sleepy lagoon
In a style that was always comely

Desert Island Discs began its broadcasting career in 1942.

30th January

This was the day they killed a king
Who thought himself above death's sting
He had a divine right
So he did not choose to fight
In the end it didn't mean a thing

Charles I was beheaded in 1649.

31st January

Philip Glass was born, on this day
Philip Glass was born, so they say
He's a minimalist
Are you digging my gist?
Philip Glass was born, by the way

In 1937.

1st February

Today is the feast of St Brigid
(And I do hope this won't bore you rigid)
It happens somehow
Her emblem's a cow
And she made damn sure milkmaids weren't frigid

Irish *Saint Brigid*, patron saint of milkmaids, is known as *St Bride* in England.

2nd February

Don't you think it's rather inauspicious
That the king of punk rock, one Sid Vicious
Should die after Nancy
(That's his long term fancy)
In circumstances somewhat suspicious?

Sid died in 1979 from an apparent overdose of heroin.
He was on bail at the time for the murder of *Nancy*.

3rd February

Every time I hear *Peggy Sue* start
That'll be the Day my eyes don't smart
I'll really never say for sure
It doesn't matter anymore
It's forever *Raining in my Heart*

Buddy Holly died tragically in 1959, aged 22.

4th February

Of a crime O J Simpson was acquitted
Perhaps they thought the jury was half-witted
But in the civil trial
They dismissed his denial
And said 'Pay up'; well, the glove kinda fitted

O J Simpson, against all the evidence, was acquitted of murder in 1995.
In 1996 a civil case was brought by the parents of the murdered women.
Damages were awarded approaching $50 million.

5th February

It was always one of my favourite treats
To go shopping with my sisters and choose sweet meats
Our Saturday passion
To cash the sweet ration
Then rationing stopped, and we bought no more sweets

Wartime rationing of sweets and chocolate ended in 1953, after an earlier attempt in 1949 badly underestimated demand.

6th February

Lancelot 'Capability' Brown
Was a gardener of certain renown
When viewing prospective facilities
He'd say 'They have their capabilities'
A technique that seldom let him down

He died in 1783. His nickname derived from habit of saying 'It has its capabilities' to potential clients which both flattered the customer's vision and implied a promising result. (Apologies for the lengthy middle lines. It was that kind of period in history.)

7th February

This was a bad day at the British Museum
They put out exhibits; they like you to see 'em
But William Mulcahy
A dull, but drunk guy
Smashed a vase like he was at the *Lyceum*

It happened in 1845. It was the priceless ten-inch Portland Vase.
The *Lyceum* in Athens was a venue for, amongst other things, military training.
I have no inkling of why this event deserves an entry in *The Book of Days*.

8th February

Let me tell you how one fine day a war was begun
The Japanese attacked from nowhere, out of the sun
The object of their fury – a
Harbour in Manchuria
So the attack in Hawaii was just a re-run

The Russo-Japanese war of 1904 began with an unprovoked attack
on Port Arthur, Manchuria.

9ᵗʰ February

Look out, there may be a red in your bed
That is just about what McCarthy said
The rest of his gist:
He'd made a long list
Although no evidence was ever read

Senator Joseph McCarthy announced the beginning of his witch hunt
in 1950. It took four years until his unfounded accusations led to him
being formally censured by the Senate for inappropriate behaviour.

10ᵗʰ February

It was a bad feast of *Scholastica*
Events were drastic (some were drasticer)
They disliked the hock
At the *Swindlestock*
And students were killed in a massacre

In 1355, students' complaints about the quality of the wine in the
Swindlestock Tavern in Oxford led to three days of mayhem in which
65 students were killed. *St Scholastica*, whose feast day this is, was a
lesser-known sister of *St Benedict*.

11th February

When the Greeks could not find the square root of two
Geometry was king, arithmetic taboo
At length came René
Who thought - and then, Hey!
Axes make geometry easier to do!

Descartes died this day in 1650. He is widely known as a philosopher, but his discovery (or invention) of coordinate or *Cartesian* geometry paved the way for modern mathematics and science.

12th February

It's a sad story, the facts are so stark
They beheaded Jane, the six day monarch
Back at home her blokes
Beheaded all the oaks
You can see them today in Bradgate Park

Lady Jane Grey, who was 'gifted' the monarchy by Edward VI was executed in 1554. If you look at a map, you will see a 'kneecap' where the M1 motorway swerves to the west to avoid her estate of Bradgate in Newtown Linford, Leicestershire.

13th February

Solzhenitsyn's expulsion by the USSR
Was something of a novelty, really quite bizarre
Dissidents should effect
A method to defect
But Alexander's exit was easier by far

On this day in 1974, adding to his celebrity in the west.

14th February

The master of spin, length, and line
Patron Saint of spinners, divine
He had a Muslim twin
One Sonny Ramadin
He is of course Alf Valentine

Those *two little pals of mine* mesmerised England
batsmen on the West Indies tour of England in 1954.
Today is the *Feast of St Valentine.*

33

15th February

This was the day the pound went metric
Everyone thought it would be quite hectic
Not metric, I mean decimal
An infinitesimal
Error – I'm really not dyslexic

We said goodbye to *shillings* (along with *half crowns, florins*, and *tanners*) in 1971. The world didn't come to an end, but serious inflation set in soon afterwards.

16th February

Castro made it to PM, as you knew
I didn't clock he was just thirty two
So he could say
To JFK
Hey you ageing politician, eff you

Castro was elected in 1959, *Kennedy* in 1960, aged 35.

17th February

There is something about great playwrights, how
They create feelings that furrow the brow
I sure learnt plenty from
Le Bourgeois Gentilhomme
Exactly what, I just can't recall now.

A work by *Moliere*, who died in 1673.

18th February

With Len it's hard to choose where to begin
Did his spy novels or his cook strips win?
Dishes that he wrote about
Did not include *sauerkraut*
For fear of a *Funeral in Berlin*?

Len Deighton was born in 1929.

19th February

Manchester United played their first game
At their stadium, Old Trafford by name
They lost four goals to three
To lads from the Mersey
Oh dear, oh dear, what a terrible shame

In 1910. That's the red side of the Mersey, of course.

20th February

Today saw both ends of Réné Dubos
The sort of fact I feel fairly few know
His life was not hypnotic
He found an antibiotic
Mainly for treatment of *gastric muco*...

He was born in 1901 and died on his birthday in 1982. His discoveries
led to the first commercially produced antibiotic. The last syllable of
the disease *gastric mucosa* seems to have gone missing....

21st February

Did someone go out on a limb
Or were people just rather dim
Why do you install
A memorial
In the town that's named after him?

The Washington Monument in Washington DC was
dedicated on this day in 1885, curiously on the eve
of the dedicatee's birthday.

22nd February

This story has a long time stood
That George had false teeth made of wood
He soaked them in port
I wouldn't have thought
That would have done them any good

George Washington was born on this (new style) day in 1732.
This story, like that of the cherry tree, is probably apocryphal.

23rd February

This was the day, to general mirth
The research team told us of the 'birth'
Of the cloned sheep Dolly
Was it progress, or folly?
Does anyone know what life is worth?

Announcement in 1997. She was actually 'born' in July 1996.

24th February

A man who was good at bits and bobs
Was born today, his name is Steve Jobs
How could he be so effete
To ban the key marked delete?
User-wise, that was one of his blobs

The founder and subsequent saviour of *Apple* was born in 1955.

25th February

Khrushchev and The Party came clean
No more would Stalin's name be seen
History exams were junked
The syllabus was debunked
Forged, to show how great Joe had been

Nikita Khrushchev denounced *Joseph Stalin* before the
Party Congress in 1956. After his death in 1952,
(the equivalent of) A level history exams were cancelled
because the students had studied unreliable information.

26th February

Today saw the running of the world's most
Famous steeplechase (or so they boast)
Ginger's equine chum
The famous *Red Rum*
Is buried beneath the winning post

The first running of the Grand National was in 1839. It is often said that
the race is a lottery. The name of the first winner was indeed, *Lottery*.

27th February

True Brit left wingers everywhere
Blow your trumpets, sound a fanfare
The Labour Party was born this day
And far too many members now say
It died when they elected Blair

Formed in 1900 from the amalgamation of the *Independent Labour Party*, the *Fabian Society*, and the *Trade Union* movement.

28th February

When you was at school I bet you was told
Today is the feast day of St Oswald
For a millennium or two
That absolutely wasn't true
So the changeover was not rushed, just bold

St Oswald, Archbishop of York, died on 29th February 992, and his feast was celebrated only in leap years, until it was changed in 1968.

29th February

The proper name for this day is *intercalary*
But using it sounds a little *la-di-dalary*
The Latin name *annus bissextus*
Summons up a different prospectus
In '68 they discovered a star that was *pulsalary*

As this day only comes round once every four years, it deserves four
limericks of its own, even if the first's a bit silly.

The first pulsar *was* discovered on this day.

Birth on the leap day must feel mean
There'll come a chance to vent your spleen
This is what you've waited for
When the rest turn sixty four
You will only be sweet sixteen

A device more used in fiction than real life.

29th February

Here is a tactic that you might like to use
Find a handsome man, and go out on the booze
Then before he gets indigestion
Bend one knee, and pop the question
Because do you know what? He cannot refuse!

So the tradition goes. It was intended for faithful but wearying girls to deal with their recalcitrant boyfriends, rather than a chance to go husband hunting.

Rossini was born on one of these rimes
He wrote operas to earn his dimes
And that is why, I'm pretty sure
In every single overture
He repeats each phrase at least four times

In 1792 on this day. *Rime* is used in its sense from that time of *crack* or *fissure.*

1st March

St David was a bishop whom Welsh folk say was meek
He was a brilliant harpist when he was at his peak
There's no truth in the rumour
(I say this with good humour)
That he looked like a daffodil but smelt like a leek

Today is the Feast Day of the Patron Saint of Wales.

2nd March

Mikhail Gorbachev trailed a humble star
The anti-Stalin, and the anti-Tsar
In the West he seemed great
But in Russia they hate
The man who lost them the USSR

Born 1931. Nobel Peace Laureate.

3rd March

The late, great conductor Sir Henry Wood
Yielded a baton like few others could
The home of the Proms
Went down to firebombs
But his tradition is in all our blood

Born 1869, the founder of the Proms, based in *The Queen's Hall* until 1940.

4th March

Listen up all y'all, while I explain ya
The origin of Pennsylvania
If you thought it was named for a pencil
Your brain is just an empty utensil
It was for William Penn – feeling brainier?

The English Quaker *William Penn* founded the state on this
day in 1681. He said to have named it in honour of his father
– although he too was called *William Penn,* so the jury is out....

5th March

In the ranking of aircraft, does one rate higher?
The *ME109* was a smash hit flier
And though *Heinkels* were smoother
They couldn't outmanoeuvre
The incomparable *Supermarine Spitfire*

The fighter plane which along with *Hawker Hurricane* won
the Battle of Britain made its maiden flight in 1936.

6th March

Il grande signor Buonarroti
Produced nothing shabby or grotty
His job in the *Sistine*
Was utterly pristine
Though he always said painting was snotty

Michelangelo di Lodovico **Buonarroti** Simoni was born 1475.

7th March

Bolero was Ravel's best work, for sure
And if he'd not composed it, what is more
We'd never have seen
Torvill and Dean
And they wouldn't have got their perfect score

Maurice Ravel was born in 1875. Ice dancing *Torvill and Dean's* perfect set of 6.0 marks in the 1984 Olympics will never be matched, because the scoring system has been changed.

8th March

As we fall asleep on our pillows
Still hearing the wind as it billows
In our prayers, as we say them
We give thanks for Ken Grahame
Or all would be still in the Willows

Kenneth Grahame, author of *The Wind in the Willows*, was born this day in 1859.

9th March

A saying suggests Boney wasn't keen
But on this night that surely can't have been
When she said
'Let's go to bed'
His answer was 'Yes, tonight Josephine'

Napoleon Buonaparte married the widow Viscountess
Josephine de Beauharnais in 1796.

10th March

The people said to AG Bell
'We do not think that it will sell
There can't be just you
You need at least two'
Bell replied 'You never can tell'

The first recognised telephone conversation happened in 1876.
You have two more messages.

Mr Watson come here I want you
                          these words are well known
As the first ever spoken (after a dialling tone)
He was in the next room
So I can only assume
Bell hadn't actually grasped the point of the telephone

Well, no-one ever thought the market for mobile phones would be children….

There was no way Bell could ever foretell
The craze for phones that are mobile (or cell)
When you look around
The numbers astound
In this ghastly social media hell

Are mobile phones a boon, or a curse?

11th March

Have you heard of Henry Tate
Every true art lover's mate
The first sugar daddy
But was he a baddy?
A billion rotted teeth to date…

Sir Henry Tate, as in *Tate* & Lyle and the *Tate* galleries
was born this day in 1891.

12th March

There are many superstitions
About death, amongst musicians
Menuhin was last heard
We said goodbye to *Bird*
Pray for no more repetitions

Yehudi Menuhin in 1998 and *Charlie 'Bird' Parker*
in 1955, both died on this day.

13th March

I'm about to do something seen as heinous
And make you pronounce the planet *Uranus*
It was spotted this day
And so, by the way
Was *Pluto*, but that fact need not detain us

Uranus was discovered in 1781, Pluto in 1930. Pluto was
declassified as a planet in 2006.

14th March

I did not know it was an actual thing
But they really did shoot Admiral Byng
I recall the Voltaire quote
Pour encourager les autres
But I took it to be the satirist's sting

British Admiral *John Byng* was executed this day in 1757,
for neglect of duty. *Voltaire* thought the decision was unjust,
and tried to intercede. He proceeded to include the incident
in his satirical, and fantastical, novel *Candide*.

15th March

And so began the very first day's play
In a sporting event alive today
The Poms met the Aussies
To find out who the boss is
Some words have been exchanged along the way

The first ever cricket test match, between Australia and England,
began in 1877 in Melbourne.

16th March

When you walk or ride a cab down *Park*
Its concrete blocks can seem quite stark
No-one much respects
The one known as *Lex*
It's *Madison* that has all the spark

Madison Avenue in Manhattan is named in honour of the fourth
President of the USA, *James Madison*, who was born in 1756.
In the twentieth century, it was a synonym for New York's
renowned advertising industry.

17th March

Saint Patrick's youngest Leprechaun
Used to rise late, feeling forlorn
With this simple trick -
A daily limerick -
He now wakes up, smiling, at dawn

Today is the Feast of *St Patrick*, Patron Saint of All Ireland.

18th March

When news of Tolpuddle was reported
Organised labour heard and retorted
But there's no mausoleum
Just a Martyr's Museum
They weren't executed, just deported

The *Tolpuddle Martyrs* were six agricultural workers who
were transported to Australia on a trumped-up charge of
conspiracy in 1834. The action precipitated the first
collective action by workers, giving birth to the trade union
movement, and eventually brought about a repeal of the decision.
Curiously, their Dorset village, which houses the museum, now lies
in a constituency where the labour candidate regular loses his deposit.

19th March

At the OK Corral, it's said
Many men were wounded or dead
But Wyatt Earp
No kind of twerp
Never chanced to stop any lead

Wyatt Earp was born in 1848. Remarkably
for a lawman, gunfighter, and professional
gambler, he was never wounded, an achievement
which contributed to his mystique.

20th March

Today is Ovid's anniversary
Born Common Era, minus forty three
I believe it is supposed
That he metamorphosed
Instead of just dying, like you and me

Metamorphoses is a narrative poem by the Roman Poet,
comprised of 11,995 lines and including 250 myths.
It provides inspirational and referential material for
the world of Western literature.

21st March

Has anyone ever sung to you this song?
In spring the nights are short as the days are long
Of autumn, I assume you were taught
The nights are as long as the days are short
They can't both be right, so which one is wrong?

I have always believed this day was the Spring Equinox (Latin for
equal night) , but I now see that it happens on Ovid's birthday.
Maybe today is the first day of spring.

(Apparently the equinox varies between 20th and 21st, but at the time
of writing, it seems to be stuck on 20th.)

22nd March

I used to know of two poets, both *kraut*
I must admit, I felt a sense of doubt
For one you only see
Is spelt out *Go-eth-e*
And *Goethe*, who you only hear about

Johann Wolfgang von Goethe died on this day in 1832.

23rd March

Today saw the birth of two English Knights
Both had 'impossible' goals in their sights
Would you believe
They're Roger and Steve?
That is Bannister and Redgrave, by rights

Sir Roger Bannister, born 1929, was the first man to run a mile in under four seconds. *Sir Steve Redgrave*, born 1962, won gold medals at five consecutive Olympics.

24th March

It measured about a thousand strokes
From each of sixteen varsity blokes
It was called a dead heat
People said 'Quite a feat
Best not re-run it, lest someone croaks'

In 1877, the boat race between Cambridge and Oxford Universities was judged to end in a dead heat for the only time.

25th March

When they met to sign the *Treaty of Rome*
There was nothing printed inside the tome
Crucial for our age
They signed the back page
What a pity they didn't just go home

The treaty which created the European Economic Community,
forerunner of the EU, was signed in 1957. According to a report
on BBC Radio's *Today Programme* in March 2007, printing delays
meant that only the frontispiece and the signature page actually
had words printed on them.

In English leases (a legal maze)
All rents are paid on the *Quarter Days*
One is Lady Day
(Today, I should say)
The fourth is Christmas, as the law says

The others are 24th June (Midsummer) and 29th September (Michaelmas).

26th March

The English have always been secretly *proward*
Of producing an artiste like Noel *Coward*
There were perhaps a little coy
When he wrote *Mad about the Boy*
But his sex life was not mentioned out *loward*

Noel Coward died this day in 1973.

27th March

Folks at the Oscars were unusually gripped
Because Billy Wilder was widely tipped
To win all three
As indeed, did he
Best producer, best director, best script

In 1960, *Billy Wilder* achieved this unique feat with his film
The Apartment. He died on this day in 2002.

28th March

Its contributors were both many and various
Uptight people said it really was nefarious
The musical play
Which opened today
This was the dawning of the age of Aquarius

The hippie musical *Hair* opened in 1968 at the Biltmore Theater, New York.

29th March

When Queen Victoria opened the Albert Hall
You'd guess her contribution was large, not small
But the Hall was subbed
The memorial clubbed
So she didn't fork out anything at all

The *Royal Albert Hall* was officially opened in 1871. The project was
already under way when Prince Albert died, so a mere change of
name was required to honour him. By contrast, the *Albert Memorial*,
which was commissioned after his death, was funded by public subscription.

30th March

Sometimes Vincent would observe, amid Flemish glowers
'They don't value the paint, let alone my precious hours'
Then on his anniversary
A somewhat more than cursory
Forty million dollars was paid for *Sunflowers*

Van Gogh was born on this day in 1853. He is supposed to have sold only one painting during his lifetime. 132 years after his birth, his *Sunflowers* became the world's most expensive painting.

31st March

Lyricists usually go to great pains
To shun poor rhymes, which a poet disdains
So I don't know why
An elephant's eye
Should be featured in the US Great Plains

Today saw the premiere in 1943 of the musical *Oklahoma!* which opens with the song *Oh what a beautiful morning*, and includes the lines *The corn is as high / As an elephant's eye And it looks like it's climbing clear up to the sky*. Not Oscar Hammerstein's best - although possibly better than *La, a note to follow Soh.*

The Almarick

1st April

On this day of all fools
I can break all the rules
So I'll have my third and fourth lines as
                          long as I possibly can
What's more, they don't even have
                – though they may try and fail – to scan
I feel like I've won the pools!

Today is also the birthday of one of England's greatest cricketers,
David Gower. Sorry David.

2nd April

Copenhagen was where Nelson famously saw
No sight of a signal bidding him withdraw
That's said to be why
We 'turn a blind eye'
But the OED dates the phrase from 1604.

In 1801, *Nelson* disregarded an order to retreat, and went on to
win the (first) *Battle of Copenhagen*.

3rd April

Whatever you say about *Also Sprach*
Composer Richard Strauss sure had the knack
Of portraying the dawn
But I believe his morn
In the Alpine air was a better crack

This is a poorly contrived link from the premiere of Stanley
Kubrick's film *2001: A Space Odyssey* in 1968. The soundtrack
begins with the portrayal of the dawn in *Strauss's* tone poem
Also Sprach Zarathrustra, which, say some pundits, is the best
ever musical representation of the arrival of the morning sun.
It is not. The start of the composer's Alpine Symphony is better.
So pundits, ASZ is not the best ever, **it's not even the best by Strauss**!

4th April

I have a dream. Do these words make your ears ring?
Do they make you want to start to dance and sing
A song by Swedes?
No, they must needs
Remind you of Doctor Martin Luther King!

The man who wrote and delivered what *The Guardian* called 'the greatest
speech of the twentieth century' was assassinated on this day in 1968.

5th April

I wonder if MacArthur is a name US kids still learn
He was held in a level of esteem few men ever earn
After his ungainly retreat
He conjured up a Jap defeat
But on this day, he went on through, but was not to return

Douglas MacArthur died in 1964. His famous statement after his initial retreat to Australia of 'I came through and I shall return' turned him into an icon for resistance against Japan.

6th April

April the sixth is the start of the tax or fiscal year
I'll tell you why - it stems from the calendar change, I fear
So if, without doubt, I say
It used to be Lady Day
I am certain I will have made myself perfectly clear

The 'lost eleven days' of the calendar reform in 1752 would have meant levying tax on a period of less than 365 days, which apparently was deemed unacceptable, so the tax year end was moved on by eleven days.

7th April

I like William Wordsworth (and his mate Sammy Coleridge)
Of English poets theirs was the most Romantic linkage
But immortality
Might have changed to fatality
If he'd wandered lonely as a cloud along Westminster Bridge

Wordsworth was born in 1770.

8th April

The *Great Western*, I would like to mention
Came from Bristol, and hence my contention
Brunel waved a wand
And she crossed the pond
Cowboy films were a British invention

The Brunel-designed *SS Great Western* began her maiden voyage
from Bristol to New York in 1838.

9th April

Don't ask me who's the best there was
Sev'riano Ballesteros!
He was the greatest
And those who protest
Are folk, like there's nowt so queer as

Inspirational Spanish golfer, born 1957. (I'm never sure
whether the correct pronunciation is buy-a *stair*-os or
buy a *steer*-os, so I've rhymed it both ways.)

10th April

This day will resonate through the land until - when?
The foundry workers heated molten steel and then
In a Whitechapel hangar
They made a great big clanger
It was a giant bell, and its name was *Big Ben*

In 1849. Neither the clock nor the tower are Big Ben. It is the name of the bell
that chimes the hour.

11th April

St Guthlac of the Fens felt left in the lurch
'Doth he seek my reputation to besmirch?'
The holy man wasn't sold
On the gift from Ethelbald
How can you be a true hermit in a church?

This is the Feast of *St Guthlac*, a fenland hermit in whose honour
King Ethelbald built Crowland Abbey.

12th April

Tin Pan Alley got a very nasty shock
When it heard the start of what we now call rock
Carefree and gaily
The great *Bill Haley*
And his Comets laid down *Rock around the Clock*

In 1954.

13th April

It's the perfect work for anyone wanting to sing
If it's not sung at Christmas, bells refuse to ring
There was much hoo-hah
With *Hallelujah*
When the audience stood up, in respect for the king

Handel's *Messiah* premiered in 1742. The following year, when King George II
stood up during the *Hallelujah Chorus*, so did the rest of the audience, thus
establishing a tradition. (Americans have the seventh inning stretch.)

14th April

April is a month for lexicographers you'll see
There's Johnson, Webster and the OED
With forty-four years'
Debate amongst peers
The third one took the longest of the three

Webster's American Dictionary of the English Language appeared
this day in 1828, having taken 22 years to compile.

The Almarick

15th April

Aboard *RMS Titanic*
There was much alarm and panic
An accident unthinkable
Rendered the famed unsinkable
No longer transoceanic

In 1912. *With five lines of equal metre,*
technically this is not a limerick, but I like it.

16th April

The Jacobite uprising wasn't to be a success
It started out well, but soon became a nasty mess
The English finally stopping 'em
Somewhere to the west of Nottingham
And then following them all the way to Inverness

The last pitch battle on British soil was at Culloden in 1746.
1,500-2,000 Jacobite soldiers were killed in one hour.

17th April

After the grief that a brutal regime inflicted
When at length people's freedom ceased to be restricted
Solidarity
Gained egality
Was this the workers' uprising Marx had predicted?

After a decade of struggle, the trade union Solidarity was recognised by the Polish government in 1989, and communist rule came to an end.

18th April

She was not the best actress we've ever seen
And definitely not any boudoir queen
But a Monegasque Prince
Made all filmgoers wince
When he took Grace away from our silver screen

Prince Rainier of Monaco married Grace Kelly in 1956, bringing a premature end to her career in films.

19th April

With forty-four years in the OUP's womb
When at last it appeared, were there cheers or gloom?
Of such a great task
It's churlish to ask
How very out of date was the first volume?

The final volume of the Oxford English Dictionary was published this day in 1928, following the first in 1884. *Dr Johnson's* (single-handed) dictionary, which appeared on 15th April 1755, took seven years.

20th April

He was one of Yorkshire's best known males
And Scottish blood put wind in his sails
So the wonder was
When he first saw Oz
Why did he label it New South Wales?

Captain James Cook sighted Australia in 1770.

21st April

As a kid I was a fighter pilot groupie
Some kids spotted trains, but I thought that was loopy
I was one of them as is
The *Red Baron's* nemesis
He was shot down today, although not by *Snoopy*

German first world war air ace Baron *Manfred von Richtofen* was shot
down in 1918. He made cameo appearances in *Peanuts* cartoons in the 1960s.

22nd April

Some Portuguese arrived in Brazil, as we name it
And so it became their colony. Oh what shame it
Fomented in Spain
On *Pinzon*, in the main
He got to the country first, but forgot to claim it.

In 1500, *Pedro Alvarez Cabral* claimed Brazil for Portugal, some three
months after the Spaniard *Vincente Yanez Pinzon* first visited it.

23rd April

When the England team goes to play in Tblisi
It's quite amazing just how surprised they can be
To see so many fans disgorge
Ten thousands of flags of St George
At away games there's often only two or three

This is the Feast Day of *St George*, who, unsurprisingly perhaps,
is also Patron Saint of Georgia (the country, not the US State.)

24th April

Sea Captain Joshua Slocum was cock-a-hoop
The day he cast off from Boston aboard his sloop
Her sails were unfurled
Around the whole world
A 75,000 kilometre loop

Starting in 1895, a single-handed journey lasting over three years.

25th April

Today saw the premiere of *Turandot*
If you've never seen it, I can tell you what
I'm sure you know
That *Vincero*
It's the one good song in the whole bloody lot

The curtain went up on *Puccini's* opera, including the now
ubiquitous *Nessun Dorma*, in 1926.

26th April

In Holy Trinity church, the Bard was on display - thus
What if some power would kindly bless, beseech and pray us
Name our own trinity
Which greats would your three be?
Mine are Shaky, Buonarroti, and Amadeus

William Shakespeare was baptised at Stratford-upon-Avon in 1564.

27th April

If you should ever lose your keys
Genuflect (go down on your knees)
Invoke St Vita
She's a world beater
She finds 'em like she's shelling peas

The Feast of *St Vita*, Patron Saint of housewives, servants,
and bakers, who is sometimes *invoked by people who
cannot find their keys* (it says here).

28th April

Wallis's *Dolphin* and Cook's *Endeavour*
Both sailed round the globe, thus famed forever
With the same nanny goat who
Was a member of each crew
Don't that make you say 'Well, I never!'?

The anonymous goat died 1772, before she could enjoy
her promised retirement in Greenwich Hospital.

29th April

Every time *I Take the A Train*
I just feel that theme and refrain
Were no fluke
Of the Duke
With his terrific musical brain

Jazz legend *Edward Kennedy 'Duke' Ellington* was born in 1899.

30th April

Today is called *Walpurgisnacht*
When all good German Burghers lacked
The will to face the night
Because of their sheer fright
Of the devils. (I'm sure it's fact)

No comment.

The Almarick

1st May

The Japs travelled the road to Mandalay
And captured the city this very day
Exactly three years on
With their potency gone
They then lost Rangoon, thus ending their stay

On this day they arrived in Mandalay in 1942, and left Rangoon,
cities in the former Burma, in 1945.

2nd May

One of the finest at the rhymster's art
I talk of the lyricist Larry Hart
But Larry, *beanery?*
How about *deanery?*
Early days, I guess. We all gotta start...

Born this day in 1895, *Lorenz Hart* wrote lyrics to *Richard Rodgers'*
songs and made a major contribution to the great American songbook.
However, in one of the earliest the lines *In a mountain greenery / where
God paints the scenery* are subsequently rhymed with *beans would get
no keener re- / -ception in a beanery* - a clever enjambement perhaps,
but would beans really get a keen reception in a beanery? A beanery
is a cheap restaurant in the US, so it would probably say something like
'Gee, not beans again!'. On the other hand, imagine the delight on the
face of a rural dean if a party of cassocked brothers pitched up at his
deanery. Still, I guess as the son of Jewish immigrants from Germany,
he wouldn't have known much about rural deans....

3rd May

The first electric train ran through the Mersey tunnel
Being electric, it wouldn't have had a funnel
Because loads of smoke
Would have been no joke
So whoever thought of it, I think they done well

The opening line is verbatim from the *Book of Days*. Was it the first ever *electric* train, the first *train* through the tunnel, or merely the first *electric train* through the tunnel?

4th May

Charles and Henry had cause to rejoice
When they agreed to sing with one voice
They went on to reveal
A new automobile
And so we first heard the name Rolls-Royce

Charles Rolls and *Henry Royce* signed their partnership deed in 1904.

5th May

They still seem to view him as an institution
With his profound failure little diminution
He made his well-known deduction
About the means of production
When what counted was control of distribution

In 2000 BBC Radio 4 listeners voted *Karl Marx* (born this day in 1818) the greatest ever philosopher despite the abject failure of his theories in practice in the USSR. From his comfortable base in London, he observed the world's leading industrial nation without noticing that workers are latent *consumers*, and that the Empire provided Britain with competition-free *customers* for its industrial output.

6th May

In fifty-four Iffley Road was the place to be
Some of the world's best milers were there for all to see
The announcer was outspoken
With a list of records broken
Before the final statement 'In a time of three...

It was once believed that running a mile in under four minutes was physiologically impossible. *Roger Bannister* proved otherwise. The announcer's voice was lost in the roar which greeted the 'three' of three minutes fifty-nine point four seconds.

The Almarick

7th May

Freude, schöner Götterfunken
What must the Viennese have thunken?
I think they took a shine
To Ludwig's number nine
Quite a few were *feuertrunken*

Beethoven's *Choral Symphony* premiered in Vienna
in 1824, although it was commissioned by the
Philharmonic Society of London.

8th May

If you should go to Helston, perchance
Go today, for it's the furry dance
A terpsichorean treat
For those with nimble feet
It's such fun, you can hear them in France

Another pagan festival (the meaning of 'furry' in Cornish perhaps)
adopted by Christianity, probably in honour of St Michael the
Archangel. Despite having his own (Michaelmas) day in September,
he is celebrated here as Patron Saint of Helston and Protector of Cornwall.

9th May

I think we should say a hurrah
For the inventor Joseph Bramah
He may sound like a chump
But he designed the pump
To get beer from barrel to bar

He patented his device in 1785.

10th May

He seemed to be a man who always knew the score
Not just of music, but of poverty and war
So *with or without you*
There'll always be U2
But have you finally *found what you're looking for?*

Bono was born this day in 1960.

11th May

In some quarters there is a suggestion
That he died of acute indigestion
We all know this much is true
The answer is forty-two
But he died without stating the question

Author of *The Hitch-Hiker's Guide to the Galaxy*, Douglas Adams died in 2001.
The indigestion is thought to have come from a contaminated towel.

12th May

Anyone who had a heart would look at me and say
'Make it easy on yourself. Just say a little pray -
-er'. I'll never fall in love again
So how can I forget you when
There is always something there to remind me, OK?

Burt Bacharach, composer of many unforgettable songs was born this day in 1929.
(Note the enjambement, Larry?)

13th May

Alison Hargreaves must have been an exceptional gal
She scaled Everest alone without oxygen *et al*
You'd think that can't be topped
But that's not where she stopped
Her death on K2 gave a new meaning to *femme fatale*

This remarkable woman achieved the feat today in 1995, aged 33. It was only the first of three Himalayan peaks she intended to climb single-handed. Ascending K2, she defied advice about bad weather, and was literally blown away.

14th May

It became David Ben-Gurion's fate
To pronounce Israel a self-ruling state
Not everyone was persuaded
The next day it was invaded
The prospects for peace have seldom been great

Since 1948.

15th May

Today saw the birth of Arthur Schnitzler
He never stood win a Pulitzer
I'm willing to bet you a tenner
It was 'cause he lived in Vienna
And was probably quite a kibitzer

He was an Austrian dramatist and novelist born in 1862. I've no
idea if he kibitzed, but he upset people with his pornographic dramas.

16th May

They are an air force legend, well-rooted in fact
The busting of the dams was an outrageous act
But was their Clermond raid
More clever by a shade
When they destroyed the plant with the canteen intact?

617 bomber squadron were assembled specially for the 1943 *Dambusters* raid
on the Ruhr valley, but then continued and excelled as a precision bombing unit
until the end of the war. In 1944 they destroyed the Michelin tyre factory in France
without harming a civilian.

17th May

Charlie Chaplin, that funny little bloke
Was buried after he had died of a stroke
Next year his body was revealed
Stolen, then buried in a field
Was that his last and greatest slapstick joke?

His body was found this day in 1978, a year after his death, having
been missing from his grave for 11 weeks.

18th May

Bertrand Russell made his parents very happy
He could count up to ten while still in his nappy
In places he's remembered yet
For the non-self-membered set
I'm sorry, but I can't make this story snappy

Russell's Paradox confounded the contemporary proposition that all of
mathematics could be derived from *set theory*. A set can be a member
of itself; for example, the set of all things bright and beautiful is clearly
a *thing bright and beautiful*. But other sets are clearly not members of
themselves. *Russell* contemplated the set of non-self-membered sets.
If this is a member of itself, then it is, by definition, also *not a member
of itself, and* vice versa. Got it?

19th May

'The monarchy is officially dead'
That's not quite what Oliver Cromwell said
I need to acknowledge
I went to his college
And somewhere therein they buried his head

In 1649, *Cromwell* declared England to be a Commonwealth.
He has a portrait in the last resting place *of his head*, Sidney
Sussex College, Cambridge. It is in the Dining Hall. It is protected
by a pair of curtains, which are formally closed prior to any loyal toast.

20th May

The murder *of* the Orient Express
Was a crime no-one would ever confess
Who would ever want to cull
A train from France to Istanbul?
The ghost of Doctor Beeching, at a guess?

The last direct train left Paris on this day in 1977.

21st May

After Amelia Earhart had flown solo across the pond
(Fifty years earlier, she'd've needed a broomstick or wand)
There piped up some tabloid snake
Asking 'Can she bake a cake?'
'For sure I can', she replied, 'but I'm not a natural blonde.'

In 1927. She didn't actually say that, but when accepting awards, she did so
'On behalf of cake bakers everywhere...'.

22nd May

To honour the maiden voyage of *The Savannah*
American folk unfurl their star-spangled *bannah*
The Irish thought she was alight
And sailed out to help with her plight
But she was merely smoking in her normal *mannah*

This was the first steam-powered vessel to cross the Atlantic, who 'set sail'
this day in 1819. To commemorate her voyage, today is *National Maritime Day*
in the US, and citizens are encouraged to fly the flag. As she approached Ireland,
onlookers saw the smoke from her funnel, and assumed she was on fire.

23rd May

He didn't just study at Eton, he was born there too
On the day the Romans emptied out their trumpets of goo
Have you an idea who he may be?
I kindly suggest you don't ask me
My answer will be plain: 'I'm sorry I haven't a clue'

Humphrey Lyttleton, son of a master at Eton College, was born in 1921.
In ancient Rome, a ceremony known as *Tubulistrium* – the cleaning of
official trumpets – took place on this day. So says the *Book of Days*.

24th May

Come gather round people wherever you roam
I got me a poetical chromosome
So spoke Robert's pa
And it's alright ma
Young Bob will soon be Bringing it all back Home

Born 1941, the *Book of Days* calls *Bob Dylan* a 'singer and songwriter'.
You could say the same of Kate Bush.

25th May

As a memorial it was very well meant
And it remains an intergalactic event
So I, Phil Dowell, say
Today is *Towel Day*
In reverence to *Zaphod*, *Ford* and *Arthur Dent*

I must admit this is not in the *Book of Days*, but the chance to use my name in a genuine rhyme in honour of one of my favourite non-musical worlds was irresistible.

26th May

'We snatched glory out of defeat'
Priestley praised the impromptu fleet
The military quirk
That took place at Dunkirk
Typically British, still upbeat

On 5th June 1940 the playwright and broadcaster *J B Priestley* proposed prophetically on radio how in years to come people would look back on this day when 'by snatching glory out of defeat, we then swept on to victory'.

27th May

This is the birthday of *Super Kraut*
The diplomat (or bullying lout)
Some say there were times
He committed war crimes
Effective, but with much moral doubt

The birthday of *Henry Kissinger* in 1923. Voted the most
effective US Secretary of State ever, there remains
considerable controversy over his career.

28th May

Today is the Feast of Bernard the Saint
He lived at altitude, but did not faint
He's best known to the masses
For a tunnel and two passes
And the dog, which is cuddly, but not quaint

Today is his Feast Day. Presumably, every other day is a dog day.

29ᵗʰ May

In 1453 Constantinople fell to the Turks
Throwing a big spanner into the Byzantine Empire's works
A million miles from the isthmus
Crosby recorded *White Christmas*
I guess that must be just one of history's meaningless quirks

Something of a disaster for the Byzantine Empire, but a 1942 triumph for
Bing, whose recording remains the all-time best-selling single by some 17m.

30ᵗʰ May

The English burnt Joan at the stake, don't forget
A deed which they had cause to come to regret
You might say it was untoward
But if you've ever been to Lourdes
You'll wish they had done the same to Bernadette

Joan of Arc was found guilty of heresy and sorcery and burnt in 1431, after
which English fortunes in the 100 years' war took a turn for the worse.

31st May

It's the birthday of *The Man with No Name*
Clint Eastwood's mum made a similar claim
Think that's a coincidence?
Let me share this confidence
I happen to know they're one and the same!

Born in 1930, *Eastwood* is probably best known for his role in
Sergio Leone's *Spaghetti Westerns*.

1st June

It was more than fifty years ago today
That *Sergeant Pepper* first taught the band to play
So it's been around for quite a while
And never really gone out of style
Rolling Stone dubbed it best ever, by the way

The *Book of Days* states the album was released on this day in 1967, though other sources differ. In 2012 for *Rolling Stone* magazine, panels of experts compiled a list of the top 500 albums of all time. *Sgt Pepper's Lonely Hearts Club Band* was number one. (Fab Four fans might like to note that *Revolver* was number three, *Rubber Soul* five, and the *White Album* ten. Some panel.)

2nd June

I will support Her Majesty through thick'n
Thin. But her presence makes my weak heart quicken
So I wasn't around
On the day she was crowned
They said that I was *Coronation Chicken*

Queen Elizabeth II's Coronation was in 1953. When she reached 2018, she became England's longest serving monarch.

3rd June

Sadly Andy Warhol is not among
The great painters on the tip of my tongue
Someone this day contrived
To shoot him; he survived
Because only the good artists die young

He was shot in 1968 by *Valerie Solonas*, a radical feminist
who believed *Warhol* had stolen her filmscript.

4th June

Few could believe that the Montgolfier *frères*
Sat in a basket and went up in the air
They took a sheep, a duck
And a rooster (for luck)
Louis XVI could only stand and stare

The *Montgolfier* brothers demonstrated their invention of the hot air balloon
in 1783. When word reached the French court, they were obliged to repeat
the show, this time with extra passengers.

5th June

Does anyone out there know what it means?
Adam Smith was born today; so was Keynes
Great students of the economy
Was it by a divine alchemy
Or was it something special in their genes?

In 1723 and 1883 respectively. Despite nearly 300 years
of economics, the public is largely ignorant of the subject,
and politicians, who may not be, ignore it.

6th June

Today was D Day (in which the D just stands for Day)
Moved from the day before, on weather forecasters' say
'The sky will be clearer tomorrow night'
Thank God what they said turned out to be right
These days, would you take their word,
                                or get down and pray?

The Allied Invasion of Normandy in 1944 depended upon a full moon and clear
skies for successful navigation and disembarkation, and was postponed from
its planned date of 5th June.

7th June

Three literati's lives came to an end
E M Forster, Henry Miller, and (my friend)
Dorothy Parker
Could there be a starker
Contrast between the sort of stuff they each penned?

It so happens that *Parker* (1967), *Forster* (1970), and M*iller* (1980) all died on this day.

8th June

Today saw the birth of Tim Berners-Lee
(I don't think he ever received a fee)
From his flow (not his ebb)
Out came the World Wide Web
From which I fear we shall never be free

The creator of the Web was born 1955.

9th June

Of the Broadway composers, my favourite is Cole
He wrote both the words and the music; few took that role
One who did was Irving
Whose fame was unnerving
But Cole was jazzier, cleverer, and much more drole

Cole Porter was born in 1891. Irving Berlin in 1888, but the latter became successful while Cole was still studying. Cole's clever lyrics often bemused censors. His early hit *Let's Do It* includes in a later refrain the lines *the most refined ladybugs do it / when a gentleman calls / moths in your rug do it / what's the use of moth balls?*

10th June

I remember it well: one forty-one point seven three
The world record Sebastian Coe set, in Italy
It stayed unbeaten for sixteen years
I wonder how many of his peers
Were brave enough to ask him what he'd eaten for his tea?

Coe's 800m record of 1981 was only bettered in 1997 by *Wilson Kepketer*, Kenyan born, but nominally a Dane.

11th June

I don't mean the writer of *Die Fledermaus*
Or any other member of that house
The man to whom my soul belongs
Finished life with his *Four Last Songs*
I refer to the composer, Richard Strauss

Richard Strauss (no relation to the Viennese) was born in Munich in 1864.
His song *Beim Schlafengehen* was played at my wife's funeral.

12th June

Bryan Allen, in his *Gossamer Albatross*
Became the first man ever to pedal across
The English channel
And that's not flannel
It was a *pedalo* (if you're still at a loss)

The American racing cyclist achieved this feat in 1979.

13th June

Some say mad King Ludwig of Bavaria
Contrarily, suffered from malaria
And then he was found
Definitely drowned
In circumstances even contrarier

He drowned mysteriously shortly after being declared insane in 1888.

14th June

Two nil up with twenty minutes left
When I hear that, I still feel bereft
Not to mention a little sobby
How dare Alf Ramsey take off Bobby
And watch the Germans in daylight theft?

Bobby Charlton's 106th and last match for England was a World Cup
quarter final in Mexico in 1970 against West Germany. He was substituted
with twenty minutes to go, whereupon the Germans scored three
goals to win the match. (Actually, he denies that this affected the
result, because *Beckenbauer*, whom he was supposed to neutralise,
scored before he was taken off. He's just being polite, as ever.)

15th June

When Philip The Good of Burgundy
Shuffled off into purgatory
Amongst his many grieving fans
Were twenty-four courtesans
I must say that sure sounds Good to me

When he died in 1467, he was known to have sired 18 surviving
illegitimate children. Why he was known as *The Good* is unclear.

16th June

Today saw the launch of President Roosevelt's *New Deal*
There was sound reason and solid faith in its appeal
The task he didn't shirk
And it appeared to work
So why are today's economies so down at heel?

Roosevelt's 1935 programme of government interventions and aid schemes literally
grew the country out of the *Great Depression* which started with the *Wall Street
Crash* of 1929. This phenomenon seems to be lost on today's politicians.

17th June

Five burglars were arrested in Washington DC
They'd broken into the Watergate Hotel (qv)
Their link-ups with CREEP
Were shown to run deep
About as scandalous as any scandal can be...

This was the start in 1972 of the Watergate Affair which ended in
impeachment of Richard Nixon. *CREEP* was the acronym for *Campaign
to Re-elect the President*, some of whose staff were a little overenthusiastic.
The suffix '-gate' is now used to turn any proper noun into a scandal.

18th June

Wellington kicked Boney's butt and tanned his hide
But it wasn't all that straightforward a ride
The sodden ground they were stuck in
Enabled Prussians to muck in
If not God, then the weather was on his side

Napoleon delayed the start of the Battle of Waterloo in 1815 because of underfoot
conditions. The delay left enough time for recently defeated, but not routed,
Prussian troops to regroup and join the battle, thus giving *Wellington* the edge.

19th June

He took a gambler's view of God's existence
That *belief* was the path of least resistance
Frenchman Blair Pascal
Was quite a rascal
If God <u>was</u> real, I bet he kept his distance

Pascal, who developed the first mathematical principles of probability, was born in 1623. In brief, his theory went that if you didn't believe in God, then if he existed, you would lose out on heaven by going to hell as a non-believer. However, if you believed, the worse that could happen without God was nothing, but the best would be heaven, because you were a believer. *This argument does not appear to bargain for God's omniscience, through which He would know that your belief was on the balance of probabilities, and not true faith.*

20th June

Is it a puzzle for you and me both
When we read about the *Tennis Court Oath?*
It was a major nuance
In the politics of France
It wasn't a stage in McEnroe's growth

It happened in 1789, something to do with how the French ruling classes managed to keep the vast majority of common people under control. Plus ça change.

21st June

This day is known as the Summer Solstice
Which word only seems to rhyme with poultice
So how do I intend
To make this effort end?
When it's gone far enough, I'll say 'Halt this'

The longest day, but not generally known as Midsummer.

22nd June

This was the institution a seafaring land deserved
Praise for its work was generous, mostly unreserved
Every British sea dog and Jack
Used its *Nautical Almanac*
Until in 1998 it went, er, unobserved

The *Royal Observatory* was founded in 1675, by Charles II. It remained in Greenwich until 1945, when it relocated via Sussex to Cambridge, where it was controversially closed.

23rd June

Today is Midsummer Eve, or Midsummer Night
Build a bonfire on a hill, and set it alight
(Myself, I have a scheme
To sleep, perchance to dream)
Then everyone walks round it clockwise (turning right)

This was one of many pagan festivals which were adapted to Saints' days, in this case *St John the Baptist*. Walking round the bonfire was said to symbolise the daily motion of the sun.

24th June

We know that we should learn from our mistakes
(*Bannockburn* ain't to do with burning cakes)
But how the deuce
Did Robert the Bruce
Beat so many English, for Heaven's sakes?

The Battle of Bannockburn ended today in 1314. It was unusual in lasting two days, a decisive battle for the Scots, but not the end of the war.

25th June

This was a bad day for the US Cavalry, I'm afraid
A hopeless mission against the odds, and
                                    what a mess they made
Poor disillusioned Colonel Custer
Lost all the troops that he could muster
Was it in emulation of the Charge of the Light Brigade?

267 of 650 Cavalry officers and men were killed at the Battle of Little Bighorn in 1876.

26th June

Herr Wilhelm Messerschmidt
Spurned the professor bit
Though he had the brains
He chose to make planes
His cars, he would confess, were schidt

Born in 1898. The cars were funny little things, maybe years ahead
of their time. No match for a *Triumph Spitfire*.

27th June

Have you like me heard of the Battleship *Potemkin*
Was it a Soviet icon? It has sounds oh so 'Kremlin'
Someone in the Russian nation
Handed me this poor translation
'In the past of revolution it has a totem been'

In 1905, there was a mutiny aboard the ship in Odessa harbour, part of the attempted revolution of that year. The event itself is best known for *Eisenstein's* silent film depicting events. By the way, you can rhyme this two ways: pronounce *been* as the quite acceptable *bin*, or use the Russian *ee* sound for the letter i.

28th June

I wonder if Lord Raglan used to grieve
It is the sort of thing that tends to peeve
A Cardigan's complete
And a Sandwich you can eat
But he was only named after a sleeve

The cardigan was named after the 7th Earl. The sandwich after the 4th Earl, a card player. The 1st Baron lost an arm and the sleeve meant he could still fight on.

29th June

When the Globe Theatre burnt down
                    they had enough doubloons
To build a new one in its place, in under thirteen moons
Then a Puritan ordinance
Banned both players and audience
The Puritans really were a miserable bunch of loons

Built in 1599, the Globe burnt down on this day in 1613, re-opening a year
later. It was closed down permanently in 1642.

30th June

Charles Blondin was a man who must have had balls
He walked a tightrope over Niagara Falls
(So he didn't play any part
In rescuing *Lionheart*)
He didn't stop at one. There were encore calls

He did it first in 1859. I wonder how they got the rope across?

1st July

In 1940, some way across the sea
Jersey and Guernsey became the invadee
But I'm in the dark
On the fate of Sark
Did it fall, or remain defiantly free?

German occupation of the Channel Islands continued
until 9th May 1945.

2nd July

It's a definite fact that Hemingway was shot, and died
His wife said it was accidental, but it's thought she lied
His sister, brother and dad
Were all similarly had
That is a good reason to believe it was suicide

It happened in 1961. I half remember a tale, which may be an urban myth, that
Ernest Hemingway's two favourite pastimes were booze and sex. He had reached
such an age, and such a depressed state, that he could only attract a woman after
a few drinks, by which time he was past performing. Hence, there was nothing left
to live for. Hemingway himself wrote 'Once writing has become your major vice
and greatest pleasure only death can stop it.'

3rd July

How fast can a duck go? Twitchers may know
But trainspotters will tell them it's not so
The *Mallard* set the pace
1-2-6 mph
Has it been beaten? – I really don't know

In 1938 the LNER's steam locomotive became the world's fastest.

4th July

This is a good day to be a Yankee Doodle Dandy
If you've got a star-spangled banner it'll come in handy
It's not pie in the sky
But the Fourth of July
Independence Day! Hunky-dory!. Clover and Candy!

And other Americanisms. It must be strange to have once been dependent.

5th July

Two records were set this day on Centre Court
After a final perhaps the most hard fought
Borg won a straight five
The first ever, dead or alive
Black man won when Jimmy Connors came up short

This is not an amazing coincidence, since Wimbledon finals were always in the first week of July. In 1974, *Arthur Ashe* beat defending champion *Connors*, with some ease. 1980 saw the famous *Borg vs McEnroe* match which was made into a feature film.

6th July

Where did you meet your best mate?
Did it feel like something great?
They say John met Paul
On the tombola stall
At a Liverpool church fete

Paul McCartney was introduced to *John Lennon* and his group, *The Quarrymen*, in 1957.

7th July

If you want to express your intrepid persona
Why not take yourself off on a trip to Pamplona?
When the bulls are abroad
There's a chance you'll get gored
And may need to give thanks to a friendly blood donor

At 8am on this day until the 14th, bull running takes place in Pamplona, when daring young men run 800m to safety, chased by six or more stampeding bulls.

I composed the above while in Naples, an experience which inspired the following:

Young Spanish men who boast the nimblest feet
Fight and kill beasts they do not want eat
It happens all over Spain
Italians, with a tad more brain
Use their matador skills to cross the street

8th July

Admiral Hyman Rickover died this day
Who the hell was he, I hear some of you say
A life under the ocean wave, he
'S the father of the nuclear navy
They told him no, but he wouldn't go away

He died in 1986, the second longest-serving US serviceman ever, who imposed his vision of nuclear-powered submarines on the US Navy almost single-handedly.

9th July

I think he strived to be
The man of destiny
Of whom people say
He took the UK
Into the EEC

Former Prime Minister *Edward Heath* was born this day in 1916. The EEC was the forerunner of the EU.

10th July

In order that people might
All sit up throughout the night
And be able to see
Transatlantic TV
Someone launched a satellite

Telstar, the first commercial satellite, was launched in 1962.
It transmitted TV pictures between the US and Europe.

11th July

US Vice President Burr
Shot Hamilton over a slur
So in the name of Burr's pride
Secretary Hamilton died
Where else would such a thing occur?

In 1804, the VP *Aaron Burr* shot and fatally wounded
the former Secretary of the Treasury *Alexander Hamilton*
after the latter had seemingly insulted him, but refused
to make a public apology.

12th July

I have criticised Oscar elsewhere
So now I think praise is only fair
You fly down the street
On the chance that you'll meet
And you meet, not really by chance – There

The lyricist *Oscar Hammerstein II* was born in 1895. These words, from the song *Hello Young Lovers* from *The King and I,* follow the lines *I know how it feels / to have wings on your heels / and to fly down the street in a trance.* Beautiful.

13th July

This is unlikely to happen again
Phil Collins sang in London, after when
He sang again in Philly
On the same day. Sounds silly?
It was *Live Aid*, and we had *Concorde* then

In 1985, *Collins* performed at the *Live Aid* concert (to raise funds for the starving in Africa) and then took a supersonic flight to the US, appearing again at the JFK stadium in Philadelphia while it was still 13th July.

14th July

The French call this *Le Quatorze Juillet*
To we Brits, it's named Bastille Day
It must have been quite a sight
For it wasn't a modest height
There were seven inmates, by the way

The *Bastille* was built of 100ft towers, and surrounded by a moat.
Although they were political prisoners, their liberation was less
significant than the sheer audacity of the raid in 1789, and the
access it provided to the arsenal stored therein.

15th July

They tell me that Anton Chekhov
Often used to bite the neck off
Bottles of beer
But I rather fear
If I'd asked him, he'd say 'Feck off'

Although it would have to have been before 1904,
when he died. Pardon my Russian.

16th July

I dreamt this unworldly enlargement
Herbert von Karajan, a bizarre gent
Decides he will marry
Conductor *Flash Harry*
And rename himself Karajan Sargent

The Austrian conductor died in 1989. *Flash Harry* was
the nickname of Englishman Sir Malcolm Sargent.

17th July

This is in memory of *Punch* magazine
The funniest weekly most people have seen
It was best known for cartoons
Clever satires, not lampoons
Contemporary, witty, and always clean

The first edition of *Punch* appeared this day in 1843. The funniest
thing about it in my younger days was that it gave every impression of
being designed for leather armchaired gentlemen's clubs, but its readership
was anything but. Misunderstanding this may have led to its failure in 1992.

18th July

Yanks pronounce *entrepreneur*
So it rhymes with words like *skewer*
They use the term more
Because what's for sure
They've got plenty, we've got *fewer*

Richard Branson was born this day in 1950. For 15 years,
when I taught *Entrepreneurial Management* on an MBA course,
he was almost invariably named as <u>the</u> British entrepreneur
by the students.

19th July

I don't know if he set out to dumbfound
But the day that George IV was crowned
It seemed not a little shabby
To ban his wife from the Abbey
What's that if not for divorce a ground?

This he did in 1821. It seems to be the King who wanted a
divorce, which she refused to grant him.

20th July

Hippies found LSD quite a lifestyle boon
(If you tripped more than once, you were a buffoon)
I went on mine
In sixty nine
And I swear I saw men walking on the moon

Which *Neil Armstrong* and *Buzz Aldrin* did on this day in 1969.

21st July

Do you know the tale of *Tam O'Shanter's* ride through hell?
It's an allegory every Scottish child knows well
'Cause every Scots kid learns
The poetry of Burns
I read some once, and was pretty sure he couldn't spell

Robert Burns died this day in 1796.

22nd July

As a career, it has a certain taint
So here's a fact that I find rather quaint
St Mary Mag
Came with that tag
And so prostitutes have a Patron Saint

This is the Feast of St Mary Magdalen, who is also patron
of pharmacists, hairdressers, and repentant sinners.

23rd July

Raymond Chandler was a master at writing crime
Stories. And Philip Marlowe's profile is sublime
I think it's common knowledge
He went to Dulwich College
As did P G Wodehouse, but not at the same time

Born 1888. *Wodehouse* was born in 1881, so they just missed each other.

24th July

Occasionally we hear tales of coppers gone astray
This criminal turned detective, it's not often that way
You probably won't clock
The name Francois Vidoçq
From a life of crime, he reformed, and built *La Sûrété*

He was born this day in 1775. An interesting character.

25th July

This used to be his Feast, but he may not have existed
So the Churches decided he should be delisted
They weren't truly thrilled to bits
On the Island of St Kitts
They thought the resolution was, shall we say, ham-fisted

Referring to the once-upon-a-time most popular Saint, Christopher, or *Kitt*.
He was 'dropped' from the liturgical calendar in 1970.

26th July

George Bernard was born, and no doubt started to yell
God help you if under his critical eye you fell
But this tends to make me roar
Although his name was *Shaw*
He titled one of his plays *You Never Can Tell*

The playwright, critic and Nobel Laureate drew his first breath in 1856.

27th July

You could say his works were multifarious
His allusions were many and various:
I am a sundial, and I make a botch
Of what is done much better by a watch
Now that, Mr Belloc, is Hilairious

Hilaire Belloc was born on this day in 1870.

28th July

Sports writers talk about the goat, now I'm (that's me)
Not acting one – it's Greatest Of All Time, see
In cricket, let's not tarry
It has to be Garry
The best batsman, best catcher, and bowler times three

Sir Garfield Sobers was born this day in 1936. In a game ripe with statistics, he is generally considered to have been the finest all-rounder ever to play the game.

29th July

Today Charles and Diana were married in St Paul's
She stumbled with his names (my pedantic brain recalls)
From then until her grave
She was the Nation's fave
And for many, Charles's treatment of her still appals

The Royal Wedding of 1981 briefly promised a bright new dawn for the Royal family. It quickly clouded over.

30th July

I wonder if he rehearsed it somehow?
Did he then stand up and take a bow?
Words came out without a hitch
'Some people are on the pitch
They think it's all over – it is now!'

Kenneth Wolstenholme's final comments on England's victory
in the 1966 World Cup have become part of our culture.

31st July

One of the best things to come out of France
Must surely be *Le Petit Prince*
Its aviating author
Retired to greener pasture
Not through natural causes, but mischance

Antoine de Saint-Exupery's plane disappeared over the Mediterranean on this
day in 1944, while on a mission for the Free French Air Force in North Africa.

1st August

The theory of phlogiston is something we now spurn
It was believed to be the substance that makes things burn
By weighing the ashes and the gas
It was shown to have negative mass
So be it, they said - some lessons, people never learn

In 1774, *Joseph Priestley* isolated a gas which turned out to be oxygen, and not as he named it, *dephlogisticated air*. It wasn't his theory, but he was a subscriber to it. People with theories and beliefs take a great deal of persuading they are wrong, whatever the evidence.

2nd August

In the New Forest, you'll find the Rufus Stone
To this day, despite tales, it remains unknown
Did the arrow deflect from a tree
Because it was simply meant to be;
It was time to remove the King from the throne?

In 1100, *William II*, known as *Rufus* was killed by an arrow reportedly shot at a stag which glanced off an oak tree and hit him in the chest. If you'll believe that, you'll believe the phlogiston theory....

3rd August

Estragon inquired of *Vladimir*
Do you think he will ever appear?
They were not to know
Waiting for *Godot*
Goes on, year after year after year

The English Language version of *Becket's* play premiered
in London in 1955.

4th August

I've never known why the USTA
Should name a court for a guy born this day
When I heard the news that the plaque was unfurled
I thought to myself, what a wonderful world
But was old Satchel Mouth allowed to play?

The *Louis Armstrong* (born 1901) Stadium is a court at the *Billie Jean King Tennis
Center* in New York. (Sorry about the 'short' lines, but the temptation was irresistible.)

5th August

I find that my search engine checks
Only three modern Sir Alecs
You'll know them all, I assume:
Bedser first, then Douglas-Home
But Guinness wins my best respects

Sir Alec Guinness died in 2000 after a most wonderful,
and versatile, acting career.

6th August

Throughout history can there have been anyone
Who was more English than Alfred, Lord Tennyson?
Theirs not to reason why
Theirs but to do and die
Of the stiff upper lip, he was the denizen

The Victorian Poet Laureate was born this day in 1809.

7th August

The Luddites would have called him a blackguard
But they were wrong about Joseph Jacquard
He invented the silk loom
And with it made fabrics bloom
For patchy colours, hold him in regard

He died on this day in 1834, giving his name to both a punch-card loom
and the fabric it creates.

8th August

Regarding the *Great Train Robbery*
There was something rather slobbery
Ronnie Biggs and his peers
Were given thirty years
A case of judicial snobbery

It took place this day in 1963, the robbers getting away with
£2 million in used notes. In hiding, they played monopoly with
real money, leaving fingerprints which ultimately convicted them.
Their sentences were longer than murderers get, surely because of
the sheer audacity of their actions, rather than its damage to humanity.

9th August

Comrade Dmitri Shostakovich
Needed to maintain a low pitch
While Stalin was alive
When he died, he could thrive
And left us a repertoire so rich

He died on this day in 1975.

10th August

Could there be a better contender
For the greatest drug-free mind-bender?
Until he gave us steel and amps
No-one had heard electric vamps
The *Strad* of guitars, Leo Fender

He was born in 1909. Did he invent the electric guitar? Who cares?

11th August

The dramatic effect was really stark
All of a sudden everything went dark
There's some getting to grips
With a total eclipse
Birds stopped singing, and dogs were scared to bark

In 1999, the eclipse was 'visible' in South West England just after 11am.

12th August

You need a fair amount of wealth
To enjoy the *Glorious Twelfth*
Though many grouse take part
It's with a heavy heart
It's not very good for their health

This is the first day of the grouse-shooting season,
itself the first shooting season to open.

13th August

Though the funeral pyre remains just an ember
Bayreuth gave patrons a night to remember
It went according to plan
So the *Ring Cycle* began
And then it ended, sometime in September

In 1876, in its specially constructed theatre, Wagner's
Kersamptkuntswerk premiered. For me, the third
syllable is pertinent.

14th August

Have you heard of Alberto Ascari?
What links him with Giuseppe Campari?
I bet your friends know
It's to do with Enzo
They both died driving a Ferrari

It's a sad fact that in 1988, the founder of F1's most iconic
marque, passed away – to join his former drivers?

15th August

When the time came for the arrival
Of *Creedence Clearwater Revival*
The fans were asleep in the mud
Their set was a bit of a dud
Woodstock was all about survival

The much-celebrated music festival of 1969 was actually
a rather miserable affair, held in poor weather, and
overrunning badly. CCR were the headline act (whose
agreement to appear set the ball rolling) but didn't come
on stage until 3am.

16th August

Have you heard of the Battle of the Spurs, perchance
Where the Englishmen led the French a merry dance?
If I may explain
Not at White Hart Lane
But in 1513, at *Therouanne*, in France

The *Book of Days* tells me that the title refers to the alacrity
with which the French retreated.

17ᵗʰ August

He was born on a mountain top in Tennessee
The greenest state in the Land of the Free
(And before your very eyes
You can watch me plagiarise)
He killed himself a bear when he was only three

Born in 1786. *Davy, Davy Crockett, King of the Wild Frontier.*

18ᵗʰ August

It must have given them quite a thrill
To launch the contraceptive pill
It took us by storm
And altered the norm
From *nice girls won't* to *nice girls will*

The Searle Drug Company launched *The Pill* on this day in 1960.

19th August

Today was the day when Groucho popped
His clogs. He just swooned and kind of dropped
To the floor. They sent for a med-
-ic, who felt his pulse and said
'Either he's dead or my watch has stopped'

In 1977, the last of the famous trio to leave us. There were five genuine Marx brothers altogether, although someone said of the fourth's appearance in a film, it was a 'case of Zeppotism'.

20th August

The top Czech Republicans say this of their troops
They're a fighting force; they are devilish in groups
The fact is they did not
Let go a single shot
In '39 or '68. They're nincompoops!

This was told to me by a Czech in his home town of *Moravsky Zizkov*, who woke up this day in 1968 but was told not to go to work. The Russians had invaded.

21st August

I cannot really say you're too much to blame
If you don't know of Keith Peacock's claim to fame
His manager thought it cute
To play him as a substitute
I don't know whether he affected the game

In 1965, Charlton's KP ran onto the pitch at Bolton as the first ever substitute.

22nd August

If you listen to it now, it may make you cringe
You would never suspect just how it would impinge
On comedy as we knew it
They killed it, and then re-grew it
I refer of course to the show *Beyond the Fringe*

The *Book of Days* states that it opened in 1960 at the Edinburgh Festival. This (common) titular error rather misses the point of the revue's title.

23rd August

I find Gene Kelly a bit of a pain
If you don't know him, then let me explain
He was a singing dancer
A somewhat pompous prancer
Who was famous for *Singin' in the Rain*

Born 1912.

24th August

In 79 CE (modern coding)
There was no sense at all of foreboding
But it was not a good day
To go and visit Pompeii
What with old man Vesuvius exploding

Pompeii was buried by the eruption.

25th August

Today saw the birth of the man they call Lenny
A composer conductor known to so many
West Side Story
Gave him glory
But he claimed it wasn't really worth a penny

Born in 1918, *Bernstein* rather resented the fame he earned from *West Side Story*, believing that he had composed many better, more serious, works. In my opinion, it was his own fault for writing such wonderful tunes.

26th August

The Battle of Crécy, as the victors would sing
'It was the English longbow that won us the thing'
This is said to be the root
Of the two-fingered salute
The archers were showing they could still pull the string

This was a victory for the English, armed with longbows, over the French, with less powerful crossbows, in 1346.

27th August

On this day there was a terrific palaver
Shown in the film *Krakatoa – East of Java*
It's actually to the west
But the producer knew best
Who cares? There were still miles of ashes and lava!

The massive eruption happened in 1883.

28th August

Today saw the births of Goethe and Tolstoy
And what say we throw in another old boy
That great English specimen
Lovable John Betjeman
The antidote to *Little Lord Fauntleroy*

Born respectively in 1749, 1828, and 1906.

29th August

This was one of the better sporting backlashes
Following one of England's earliest hashes
The *Sporting Times* did its bit
With this sarcastic obit
'The body will be cremated and the ashes...'

...taken to Australia.' After a 'disastrous' defeat in 1882.

30th August

'Like a cannon ball bouncing off tissue paper'
That's how Ernest Rutherford described his caper
The method was dubious
Which revealed the nucleus
Of scientific progress, this was a shaper

Noble Laureate *Ernest Rutherford* was born in 1871 in Brightwater, New Zealand.
He performed his most famous work *after* receiving the Nobel Prize.

31st August

The Playwright Bertold Brecht breathed new life
Into Gay's tale of demi-monde strife
The music was by Kurt Weill
Who seldom makes people smile
But this time he gave us *Mack the Knife*

Suitably decadent, *The Threepenny Opera* premiered in Berlin in 1928.

1ˢᵗ September

In London's Cripplegate a church you will find
That of St Giles, the Patron Saint of lame mankind
He was a Greek, by some chance
A recluse living in France
Who was nourished by a kind lactating hind….

His feast day. Oh yeah I know… but the hind is included in Edinburgh's Coat of Arms, a city whose cathedral is dedicated to *St Giles*.

2ⁿᵈ September

I haven't the space to repeat Evelyn's narration
Witnessing London's great conflagration
Let me merely document
The height of the Monument
Is its distance from the start of the mass cremation

In 1666. The 202ft Monument was designed by Sir Christopher Wren, along with St Paul's Cathedral and fifty churches.

3rd September

We were told that Ho Chi Minh died on this day
Guess what the New York *Daily News* had to say:
The headline *Ho becomes a good red.*
A red is only good when he's dead
(And they kinda thought he'd never go away)

Another colourful event from the summer of 1969.

4th September

For me, Anton Bruckner's symphonies are a hit
But I do admit they tend to go on a bit
While writing number nine
He was called by the Divine
No finale; not even God could have sat through it

Bruckner was born this day in 1824. When he died in 1896, it seemed he had fallen to the curse of the ninth symphony, which Mahler made such a fuss about. In fact, like Mahler, it wasn't actually his ninth. He wrote two 'study symphonies', known as numbers 0 and 00.

5th September

This is the day when scholars debate
Whether *Tsar Peter* was all that *Great*
Not a hirsute man cheered
To pay tax on his beard
Is shaving a concern of the State?

The tax was imposed by Peter the Great in 1698, to encourage
the westernisation of Russian fashion.

6th September

On Princess Diana's final farewell
Over 2 billion watched, so I've heard tell
Her brother's address
Lambasted the press
And much of the House of Windsor as well

An estimated 2.2 billion people watched live on television the
funeral of *Diana, Princess of Wales* at Westminster Abbey in 1997.
Elton John's single *Goodbye England's Rose* sold 33m copies.

7th September

Today is the birthday of Good Queen Bess
Who claimed the throne with the State in a mess
She took to the task with ardour
Thrashing the Spanish Armada
And ruled her subjects with grace and largesse

Er, relative to what went before, that is. Born 1533, Queen from 1558 to 1603.
Her successor James was her cousin twice removed. As he was known as 'the
wisest fool in Christendom' perhaps that was by men in white coats.

8th September

In 1968 tennis history was made
When the first United States Women's Open was played
The woman who won the thing
Disposed of Billie Jean King
She was none other than our own Virginia Wade

This was the US start of what is known as the 'open era'. Prior to this date,
these were known as the US National Championships.

10th September

Arnie was blessed with great skill, and quite a shrewd brain
With help from McCormack, he was the guy who in the main
Made use of his fame
To turn a good game
Into a multi-million dollar gravy train

Arnold Palmer, the world's first golfing superstar, was born in 1929. His celebrity was great enough to create a new industry, that of Sports (star) Management, started by *Mark McCormack* of IMG.

11th September

When the Russians abandoned *Sevastopol*
I wonder what was the formal protocol?
Did they get down on their knees
And then hand over the keys
Or just leave when they ran out of alcohol?

During the Crimean war in 1855, the Russian stronghold was abandoned after a year-long siege.

12th September

Henry VI was blessed with both vision and prudence
He approached education with vim and exub'rance
For his college known as King's
(That chapel where the choir sings)
He set up Eton, to provide a stream of students

Eton College was founded in 1440, actually a year before King's. It was originally a charity to provide free education for 70 poor boys. Hence a 'public' school. Children of wealthy families had their own governors and governesses.

13th September

I think we should all complain
About Michel de Montaigne
Without the bloody *essai*
School *faire* would be more *laissez*
Writing essays is a pain

The inventor of the *essai* died at his eponymous chateau in 1592.

14th September

Today, do not go wood cutting, nay!
Is that because stags are rutting, pray?
For most deer stocks
That's post equinox...
This is the first Devil's Nutting Day!

The second is in a week's time. This is thought to be an
attempt to discourage young people from hazelnut gathering,
along with other harmless pursuits, in the woods. Especially on Sundays.

15th September

The new railway opened with some novelty
And pretty soon, came its first casualty
An MP who crossed the track
Got an engine in his back
He died; the *Rocket* incurred no penalty

In 1830, at the inauguration of the Liverpool to Manchester
railway, William Huskisson, MP for Liverpool, was injured by
a passing train pulled by Stephenson's Rocket, and died later
of his injuries. The trains in the inaugural party had stopped for
water, and the passengers alighted. Huskisson spotted the Duke
of Wellington and crossed the track to speak to him.

I suppose it had to happen sometime.

16th September

Were the Pilgrim Fathers, on their maiden
Voyage, at the same time Plymouth Brethren?
They sailed from, and then landed at
Plymouth. So how about that?
But they started from Holland, at Leiden

The *Mayflower* set sail from Plymouth on this day in 1620. The
Pilgrim Fathers were a group of English Puritans originally from
Lincolnshire, who had relocated to Holland to avoid persecution.
They were granted territory in Virginia. They missed the target by
about 500 miles.

17th September

I would like to make a little contribution
To the feast day of the US Constitution
Regarding mine
I'm generally fine
But it's better after my morning ablution

The Constitution was signed this day in 1787, is naturally
commemorated every year.

18th September

This was the day when Jimi Hendrix was late
Terminally so, such was his dreadful fate
He may have spent his last days
Inside a *purple haze*
But was he *experienced*, at twenty-eight?

His body was found in a flat in Lansdowne Crescent, W11, in 1970.

19th September

Krushchev had quite a temper, didn' he
Not often in life does a kid see
A man of his age
Fly into a rage
When told he couldn't go see Disney

But this happened in 1959 when the Soviet Premier was told
he could not go to Disneyland 'for his own safety'.

20th September

In the famous Houston Astrodome in Texas
Ms King played Riggs in the Battle of the Sexes
King employed her gain
To launch a campaign
For Riggs it was a blow in the solar plexus

In 1973, Billie Jean King accepted a challenge from Bobbie Riggs, a former men's champion but now aged 55, to play a match for $100,000. Riggs had recently beaten Margaret Court, and was boasting. King won a best of five sets match in three straight, in an event which is said to have kick-started her campaign for equal prize money for men and women (but not best of five matches). The US National Tennis Center in New York now bears her name.

21st September

Gustav Holst is famous for his *Planets Suite*
In 2000, The Halle thought it was neat
To add a piece for *Pluto*
But it was not *sostenuto*
Six years later, *Pluto* was declared a cheat

Holst (an Englishman despite his name) was born in 1874. Pluto was discovered before he died, but he showed no interest in adding it to the suite. It was subsequently reclassified as a dwarf planet.

22nd September

A coal mine has always been a place to fear
For events like those at Gresford, most severe
265 miners' lives
Leaving children, and hapless grieving wives -
And people put up signs *No Giant Turbines Here*

This happened in a mine near Wrexham in 1934, when an explosion
was followed by a fierce fire. Anyone who has ever lived in a coal mining
area is at a loss to understand the namby-pamby nimby attitude that
causes people to object to potentially planet-saving wind turbines.

23rd September

His success should never have been scored
For how can a method be assured
To test through scientific schemes
His interpretation of dreams?
Farewell you charlatan, *Sigmund Fraud*

He died this day, in 1939 in London. Although he only came to
England in 1938, there is a Freud Museum in Hampstead.

24th September

They asked him which was better, the record or the gold?
He replied 'The medal. I'll still have it when I'm old'
How wrong can you be, Ben?
Remember what happened then?
He failed a drug test, and was left out in the cold

Canadian *Ben Jonson* finished first in the 100 metres at the Seoul Olympics on this day in 1988, in a new world record time. He then tested positive for anabolic steroids, the record was scratched and the medal stripped.

25th September

When Harald met Harold he must have reckoned
(That's Harald the Third but Harold the Second)
He'd got the thing nailed
But Harold prevailed
He hurried back south; Willy the Conk beckoned

This was the *Battle of Stamford Bridge* in Yorkshire in 1066. The Dane *Harald* was supported by his brother *Tostig*, but the Saxon *Harold* won the battle against the odds, slaying both his opponents. He then had to get his troops back to *Hastings* for a date on 14th October.

26th September

Tonight, it may be that nostalgia calls
There's a place for us, our seats in the stalls
We'll be there to see a
Show about *Maria*
And Tony, and the tale that still enthrals

West Side Story premiered in New York in 1957, changing
the face of musicals for ever.

27th September

The Warren Report stated there was no conspiracy
But Americans don't like events they don't 'wannabe'
They tax their collective brain
In an effort to explain
The same for nine eleven; should we call that lunacy?

The Commission of Inquiry into the death of President Kennedy was led by
Earl Warren (I had no idea the US had an aristocracy) and reported this day
in 1964. Some American people still believe otherwise, as they do of 9/11.
After all, America is God's country which controls the World, doesn't it?

28th September

Our tribute to the monarch of our nation
Was given its first public incantation
After the Scots gave George II
Very much more then he had reckoned
So maybe it was sung in desperation

It premiered in the Theatre Royal in Drury Lane in 1745, shortly after the King's troops had been defeated at Prestonpans.

29th September

Michelangelo Antonioni
Was the single one and onlyonly
Film director who
Used a blind film crew
I'm sorry, that's pure baloneyoney

The director of, for example the 60s cult film
Blow Up, was born this day in 1912.

30th September

I'm just sitting watching flowers in the rain
That was the opening, popular refrain
On the new radio station
To protect both Beeb and Nation
From nasty pirate ships anchored in the main

BBC Radio 1 was launched on this day in 1967. DJ Tony Blackburn
played the *The Move's* chart record of the time.

1st October

There was a time when the land was lacking
A broadsheet rag where the news was cracking
There were many views
Of the *News of the Screws*
'Til it closed down because of phone hacking

The *News of the World* newspaper first appeared on this day in 1843.

2nd October

Richard of York gave battle in vain
On Bosworth field he was at length slain
In history, this closes
The Wars of the Roses
England was never the same again

1485 is generally considered the end of the Middle Ages.

3rd October

This procedure just came into force:
If your ship should lose track of its course
And is in distress
Transmit SOS
And give thanks to good old Sam Morse

Agreed in 1906 at the Berlin Radiotelegraphic Conference.

4th October

The people weren't sure about Frankie
They thought he was possibly cranky
It's rather absurd
To preach to a bird
And other such weird hank-panky

Feast Day of St Francis of Assisi.

5th October

I wonder if there has ever been
Anything quite so unforeseen -
Something completely different
And utterly irreverent -
When the Pythons appeared on screen?

First broadcast in 1969 of *Monty Python's Flying Circus.*

6th October

Its impact on Paris was huge
Amongst patrons, it caused a *deluge*
As every man ran
To see the can-can
Danced at the new *Moulin Rouge*

The famous theatre opened in 1889.

7th October

I don't think that I'm a stuffed shirt
But don't you reckon it must hurt?
(Though everyone sez
It didn't bother Des)
To be named for a dancer's skirt?

The South African Anglican Archbishop and Nobel Peace
Prize winner *Desmond Tutu* was born in 1931.

8th October

The Mayor made it known in Chicago
That he'd sanctioned a media embargo
'It ain't good for the town
If folks hear it's burnt down
And all we've got left's a farrago'

The Great Chicago Fire of 1871.

9th October

The French know him simply as *Jacques*
The comic who just had the knack
But I wonder if *Hulot*
Ever really knew, though
The millions of sides he would crack?

The birth of comic film actor and director Jacques Tati in 1908, creator of *Monsieur Hulot's Holiday.*

10th October

He was never ceremonious
You can't call his style harmonious
You might say Mister Monk
Anticipated Punk
So thank you for that, Thelonious

Innovative jazz pianist and composer, born in 1917.

11th October

At the *Meditrinalia*
With Roman paraphernalia
They tasted the wine
And judged it was fine
If it engorged their genitalia

The ceremony at which the new season's wine was first tasted.

12th October

Columbus set sail from Las Palmas
And made landfall in the Bahamas
This tale is embellished
For what he most relished
Was hope he could buy fresh pyjamas

Columbus made landfall in 1492, arriving at the
Bahamian island of San Salvador.

13th October

In Turin Cathedral they wondered
Perhaps the Archbishop had blundered
He was not at all proud
To announce that the shroud
Carbon-dated to round thirteen hundred

In 1986, the Archbishop announced that carbon dating showed
the *Turin Shroud*, believed to bear an imprint of Christ's face,
was in fact mediaeval.

14th October

Today was when the Anglo-Saxon clan
Fell foul of that Norman Conqueror man
The year always sticks
It's ten sixty-six
When history, as we know it today, began

The Battle of Senlac, near but not actually in Hastings and
now called Battle, put England under Norman control.

15th October

There were other folks surely much keener
To sail into Jamestown (St Helena)
But Napoleon knew
He'd met his Waterloo
You could tell from his gen'ral demeanour

Napoleon arrived at his final resting place, an island in the
South Atlantic, in 1815

16th October

This was the birthday of the child
The world would know as Oscar Wilde
Everyone would admit
His magnificent wit
But his taste for men was reviled

In 1895 *Oscar Wilde* was imprisoned in Reading Gaol
for gross indecency.

17th October

In bygone days the Fair of St Audrey
Heard language that was vulgar and bawdry
The reason, so I'm told
Was the goods that were sold
Were substandard, or as they say, tawdry

The Fair used to be held in Ely, and is the origin of the word tawdry.

18th October

The venetian artist Canaletto
Painted scenes from *St Marks* to the *Ghetto*
When he shows a canal
(And this may seem banal)
Why doesn't he feature a *vaporetto*?

Canaletto was born this day in 1697. The Venetian steamboat known as vaporetto was not invented until the 19th century.

19th October

I wonder what happened in the Court of Law
That saw the conviction of the Guildford Four?
I bet they got sloshed
The day it was quashed
D'you think we can trust it will happen no more?

Four people who were imprisoned for their part in the Guildford bombing
of 1974 finally had their convictions overturned in 1989.

20th October

This was the day when all the masses
Felt jealous of Mr Onassis
He did marry Jackie
But it was all rather tacky
And treacly as first grade molasses

Greek ship-owner *Aristotle Onassis* married *Jacqueline,*
widow of President John Kennedy in 1968.

21st October

I'll tell you, for what it is worth
1940 was short of mirth
The Blitz reeked of doom
And to add to the gloom
They announced Geoffrey Boycott's birth

The birth one of England's best cricketers, later becoming
The marmite of cricket pundits.

22nd October

A Frenchman once thought it was rather wise
To shun the award of a Nobel prize
Saying 'I made the Art
That's inside Jean-Paul Sartre
I won't have it institutionalised'

Sartre gave his reasons for declining the Nobel Prize for Literature in 1964.

23rd October

The much-vaunted *Afrika Korps*
Turned out to be really quite poor
They felt all the pain
At El Alamein
And watched Monty's eminence soar

The start of the Battle of El Alamein in North Africa,
and turning point for Allied fortunes, led by Field
Marshal Montgomery in the Second World War.

24th October

The source of leaders' frustrations
And many despots' irritations
It went live
In '45
Of course, it's the United Nations

The UN Charter was ratified by participating nations
on this day, which is now United Nations Day.

25th October

I think myself accursed I was not there
(And I am glad that I have shoes to wear)
For this is Crispin's day
When all the cobblers say
We beat the French at Agincourt, so there

The Battle of Agincourt took place in 1415 on the *Feast of St Crispin*, Patron Saint of cobblers, and cited in Shakespeare's Henry V.

26th October

Many people make this mistake
Thinking 'twas Hereward the Wake
So just let me state
It was on this date
That King Alfred burnt his last cake

Saxon *King Alfred* died in 899, who successfully repelled invading Danes from Wessex. He was mythically famous for failing to keep watch as requested over a woman's cakes as they were cooking.

27th October

I *did* go gentle into that dark night
And what I got was a really stark fright
What I took for carbuncles
Were in fact Christmas uncles
By themselves still not the most pleasant sight

Dylan Thomas, Welsh poet and broadcaster was born in 1914.
In *A Child's Christmas in Wales*, he notes that there are always
uncles at Christmas, with enormous midriffs

28th October

John Harvard's gift was immense
A College to teach common sense
It isn't in Boston
A fact that's not lost on
Alumni Cantabrigens

The English-born priest bequeathed the legacy which
founded Harvard College in Cambridge, MA in 1636.

29th October

When Mozart sat down at the piano
To sing of the Don (*tutti sanno*)
They all said goodbye
To *Non piu andrai*
To sing *La ci darem la mano*

These are arias from Mozart's operas *The Marriage of Figaro* and its successor, *Don Giovanni,* which premiered on this day in 1787. *Tutti sanno* means 'everyone knows'.

30th October

You would not believe such a thing
Could ever be done by a king
But *Vic' Em' il tre*
D'Italia il re
Put fascism into full swing

In 1922 King Victor Emmanuel III asked fascist leader Benito Mussolini to form a government. He was the last ever Italian king.

31st October

Today is the eve of All Hallows
When nasty things happened with gallows
And witches and rakes
Were burnt at their stakes
And now – I just toast my marshmallows

A once pagan festival of the supernatural became the Christian Eve of All Saints, or All Hallows. To hallow means to make holy, as in the Lord's Prayer 'Hallowed be Thy Name'.

1st November

Don't mix up Benvenuto Cellini
With a man called Vincenzo Bellini
It seems Benvenuto
Was fond of *prosciutto*
Vincenzo liked cheese in his *tortellini*

Cellini, of whom Berlioz *wrote an opera*, was a sculptor and goldsmith who was born this day in 1500. Bellini *composed* operas, most notably *Norma*.

2nd November

It's hard to believe that before this day
(Back in nineteen eighty two, by the way)
There were amazingly only three -
One independent, two BBC -
TV channels covering the UK

Channel 4 began broadcasting on this day.

3rd November

I know this may sound quite absurd
It was on November the third
(Keep a straight face)
A dog went to space
With no-one to clean up after her

The USSR sent into space a dog called *Laika* in a sputnik.
She didn't survive.

4th November

At their first Royal Show, a tad Liverpoolery
The Beatles act included some tomfoolery
John's words struck a chord:
'In the cheap seats, applaud
And the rest of you just rattle your jewellery'

This was the Royal Variety Performance of 1964, where the *Fab Four*
once again distinguished themselves from the mob of beat groups.

5th November

When William of Orange landed at Torbay
Did anyone tell him it was a long way
To get to Buck House?
Whence he and his spouse
Could ascend to the throne the following May

He did indeed, in 1688. Perhaps given the date, he was giving parliament a wide berth.

6th November

When conducting a band he held on to his head
His reason was as follows, or so it is said:
Lest it fall off
(*Un trait Romanoff*)
When at last he died, it was with him in bed

Tchaikovsky believed, as did many aristocrats at the time, that parts of his body were insecurely attached. He died this day in 1893, his head and body still firmly connected.

7th November

If you check the facts I think you'll find
Today was a bad day for mankind
The October revolution
Began its persecution
Russia was always a step behind

It was actually 25th October 1917, but in the old style calendar (so it says, though it doesn't add up) which Russia used long after the rest of Europe.

8th November

There was a famous Russian barman known as Mollie
His chat lines were good, but to drink his drinks was folly
Although they weren't corrosive
His cocktails were explosive
To sniff one was enough to knock you off your trolley

Vyacheslav Molotov, a Soviet statesman who died 1986, is best remembered for his improvised revolutionary weapon, the *Molotov cocktail*.

9th November

He went to the White House the youngest of all
Ich bin ein Berliner his rallying call
Then to our dismay
We lost JFK
But twenty nine years on, they took down the wall

The demolition of the Berlin Wall began on the 29th anniversary of
John Fitzgerald Kennedy's election to the US Presidency.

10th November

Two hundred thousand copies went in a day
Paperbacks don't usually sell in that way
Constance and *Mellors*
Became best sellers
If there'd not been a trial they'd have stayed passé

The unexpurgated Penguin edition of *Lady Chatterley's Lover* sold its
entire print run on this day in 1960, after the publishers were acquitted
in an earlier, well-publicised trial under the Obscene Publications Act.

11th November

We remember the poppies in their vast throngs
And we sing once more those reverential songs
A century has come and passed
Since *The War that would be the Last*
But Nations still go for it hammer and tongs

The *Armistice* ending the First World War was signed on the
eleventh hour of the eleventh day of the eleventh month of 1918.

12th November

They said that, as kings went, he was astute
He told his flock he wasn't all that cute
But still, he tried
To hold back the tide
Which made him look like a stupid Cnut

English, Danish and Norwegian King *Knut Sveinsson*, also
known as *Cnut* or *Canute* died on this day in 1035.

13th November

They must have thought it ever thus
The segregation on the bus
But Rosa Parks
Got off her marks
And the courts ruled it *sine jus*

The US Supreme Court ruled that bus segregation in
Montgomery and all of Alabama was illegal on this
day in 1956, 347 days after *Rosa Parks* refused an
order to relinquish her seat for a white person.

14th November

This was the day when young Nellie Bly
Set off around the world. Thus would she try
To beat Phileas Fogg.
She went the whole hog
Remarking 'The time just seemed to fly'

This was the pseudonym of *Elizabeth Cochrane Seaman*, a 22 year
old journalist, who accomplished the feat in 73 days in 1888.

15th November

As we saw the flames take hold we trumpeted with glee
Then we sang the chorus from Atlanta to the sea
What a pretty town
To choose to burn down!
This has gotten as good as a civil war can be!

In 1864, General Sherman's troops captured and burnt down Atlanta, beginning
the 'March to the Sea' commemorated in the song *Marching through Georgia*.

16th November

The story goes that the great Clark Gable
Once went out with gorgeous Betty Grable
They found a speakeasy -
Judged suitably sleazy -
Where she then drank him under the table

Film Actor *Gable* died on this day in 1960. There is no truth in this
story, but frankly, I don't give a damn.

17th November

Today I am going to fix on
The words of President Nixon
According to my book
He said 'I'm not a crook'
Did you think that we're all thick, son?

Nixon's full declaration in 1973 was 'People have got
to know whether or not their president is a crook.
Well, I am not a crook.'

18th November

This was the day when Hans Blix went back
For one final thorough search of Iraq
Everyone knew –
Though it wasn't true -
There were (no) hidden weapons he could track

Blix led the UN Weapons Inspectors in their attempts to find
weapons of mass destruction in Iraq, which, despite
'everyone knowing' they existed, failed to materialise.
After this final effort in 2002, Blix reported their
non-existence to the UN Assembly. The US nevertheless
declared war on Iraq, supported by the UK.

19th November

Edson Arantes do Nascimento
Kept this shirt as a lasting memento
It was the one he wore
For his one thousandth score
A kind of footballing *sacramento*

This happened in 1969. Playing for *Santos*, the player
was better known as *Pele*.

20th November

It must have been strange to live in a land
Blacked out so you cannot see your own hand
So imagine the sense of relief
(Maybe mingled with some disbelief)
When they switched the lights back on in The Strand

The lights in *The Strand* and *Piccadilly Circus* were switched back on in 1944,
presumably to demonstrate London's final immunity from the *Luftwaffe*.

21st November

The commune of *Ferney* will always lament him
He was outspoken, though they tried to prevent him
Voltaire, I assume
Was his *nom de plume*
If he'd not been born, we'd've had to invent him

Born in 1694, Francois-Marie Arouet spent much of his life in the *Genevoise* commune now called in his honour *Ferney-Voltaire.*

22nd November

'You only live once (and that kind of stuff)
But if you live it right, once is enough'
One of the very best
From the unique Mae West
Who talked it smooth, and may have liked it rough

Mae West died on this day in 1980.

23rd November

It happens a lot when my brain isn't workin'
That I get mixed up between Parkin and Perkin
I think Parkin's a cake
But Perkin was a fake
Who they put in the tower, to go bezerk in

Perkin Warbeck, a Flemish impostor who claimed to be Richard, Duke of York, was executed on this day in 1499.

24th November

I wonder if the world was ready
To welcome a talent so heady?
Creatively Promethean
With a rhapsody too Bohemian?
Too soon we said good bye to Freddie

Freddie Mercury died on this day in 1991.

25th November

The plot of *The Mousetrap* is really cunning
And here is a fact which you may find quite stunning
The play has been seen
Longer than The Queen
Has reigned. And you know, I think it's still running

The play opened in 1952, six months before Elizabeth II's coronation.

26th November

Nothing delights a skilful shopper more
Than a bargain at an upmarket store
All Yanks living
Love Thanksgiving
But some now love Black Friday even more

Thanksgiving Day became the USA's first public holiday in 1789.

27th November

Celsius is a man of world-wide renown
But when I read his paper, I had to frown
I liked his general scheme
Of fixed points for ice and steam
But when he announced them they were upside down.

Anders Celsius was born in 1701. His original temperature scale had
freezing at 100, and boiling at zero. The term 'mad scientist' comes to mind.

28th November

I don't think I'll ever understand
How a *tyger* can burn like a brand
But let me not forsake
The name of William Blake
God forbid my sword sleep in my hand

The English mystic was born in 1757.

29th November

All music lovers, near and far, missed
The Beatle whose play they called star-kissed
No-one bears comparison
With George Harrison
The greatest ever lead guitarist

George died in 2001. He was lead guitar in the greatest ever
ensemble, which is near enough.

30th November

The first ever case of man flu
Is said to have been St Andrew
He got up to high jinks
On his eponymous links
As a Patron Saint, you can do

Today is *St Andrew's Day*, Patron Saint of Scotland.

The Almarick

1st December

In Napoleon's time it was a romance
At length, it surely didn't happen by chance
Borers from each nation
Reached their consummation
That moment England was connected to France

Napoleon first imagined such a tunnel. Nearly two centuries later, in 1990, tunnellers from England and from France connected beneath the English Channel. They shook hands, exchanged flags, and drank champagne – the French created the wine, but the English invented the bubbles.

2nd December

Austerlitz was no *nom de gare* chosen by chance
It's where Boney led the Russians a song and dance
I give one of my smiles
That Napoleon had piles
Otherwise Waterloo station would be in France

The Battle of Austerlitz took place in 1805 in the present day Czech Republic. It is said that Napoleon's piles led him to make poor decisions at Waterloo.

3rd December

Edwina Currie was what you call a tabloid gem
A source of verbal trouble spin doctors could not stem
She announced on telly
Eggs were salmonelly
But stranger still was her affair dalliance the PM

In 1988 *Edwina Currie* caused an outcry, leading to her resignation as
Health Minister two weeks later. It later emerged that she and John
Major had shared a romantic liaison.

4th December

They never knighted the great Benjamin Britten
Do you think it was 'cause he was clearly smitten
With one Peter Pears?
(That damned pair of queers!)
They shacked up long before the law was re-written

Who knows? – but Michael Tippett, arguably the second finest British
composer of his era was knighted in 1966. *Britten* was given a life peerage
in 1976, the last year of his life.

5th December

Mozart's early biographers commonly misbehave
With the myth he was buried in an unmarked pauper's grave
Was the *Requiem* his own?
Well, that will never be known
But go and see his tombstone in Vienna, should you crave

Mozart was buried in a citizen's grave, the highest status after the aristocrat's vault.
This was, as was usual at the time, unmarked, but if you now go to St Marx cemetery
in Vienna, you will find it.

6th December

John Brown's body continued mouldering in his grave
History isn't sure if he was loony or brave
Perhaps it gave a little jerk
When he had done his lifetime's work
No American would henceforth ever be a slave

John Brown campaigned, often violently, against slavery. He was hanged in 1859.
On this day in 1865, Congress ratified the 13th Amendment, abolishing slavery.

7th December

Without hint of a cough or a sneeze
Out of nowhere came the Japanese
To set America mourning
Without a trace of warning
The US response would cause unease

Japan launched a unilateral attack on Pearl Harbor in 1941,
bringing the USA into World War II. It ended when, also
without warning, atomic bombs were exploded over Japan.

8th December

Do you remember the Falklands War?
Will you please make quite certain you're sure
It was in 1914
The victory was routine
Why did they battle so far offshore?

The British Navy defeated the German fleet, in 1914, in the South Atlantic.

9th December

I wonder if the perpetrators feel sorry
For the creation of the juggernaut-sized lorry
That trundles across our screens
Starring was-nots and has-beens?
I refer of course to the Soap known as Corrie

The first episode of Coronation Street was broadcast on this day in 1960
– an odd choice for the launch of the world's longest running soap.

10th December

It's held that the first ever flight to down under
Was by Amy Johnson, that high flying wonder
But that is merely a myth
It was the brothers Smith
Who did it before her and stole Amy's thunder

The Australian brothers Ross and Keith set off in 1919, completing the journey
in 28 days. In 1928, *Bert Hinckler* made the first solo flight. Two years later,
Amy completed the first solo flight by a woman, taking 19 days.

11th December

I understand the facts were widely known
Which in the end made Teddy quit the throne
It was plainly indisputable
His fiancée was unsuitable
Why didn't he take Mrs Simpson on loan?

King Edward VIII abdicated on this day in 1936.

12th December

I don't know if they did tell Marconi
That his wireless idea was a phoney
But he had no idea
Of the ionosphere
And his theories, it's true, were baloney

Marconi thought that radio waves travel in straight lines,
so how did he expect his signal to follow the curvature of the
earth? We now know the signals were reflected by the ionosphere,
which was not part of the plan. (I heard that on the radio sometime,
so it may be a little garbled.)

13th December

'Your majesty, Drake is of a mind
Do you think he should be so inclined?'
'I know full well he can
Rename the *Pelican*'
That's why it's known as the *Golden Hind*

Sir Francis set sail to circumnavigate the earth in 1577 in the
Pelican. He renamed it after his sponsor's crest the following year.
He did not ask the Queen's permission.

14th December

Of quantum mechanics Einstein spoke
We must acknowledge that Holstein bloke
I think we should thank
The brilliant Max Planck
But is it useful, or just a joke?

Planck announced his theory in 1900. It is held in some quarters
that if you manage to understand it, you go mad.

15th December

It wasn't just one of those nights
There were none of the usual fights
'We now agree
All men are free'
When Congress passed the Bill of Rights

The rights of American citizens (though not slaves) were ratified in 1791.

16th December

It wasn't a party with nibbles and snacks
In case you don't know them, here are the facts
Three shiploads of tea
Were dumped in the sea
Which brought forth the so-called Intolerable Acts

In response to the Boston Tea Party in 1773, the British Government imposed draconian – 'intolerable' – restrictions on Massachusetts, ultimately leading to the War of Independence.

17th December

Saturnalia begat Christmas, remember
Around this time in each and every December
Crackers were cracked
And morals relaxed
Which may account for all the births in September

The Roman winter festival began on this day.

18th December

Peel's manifesto may have been fine
In shaping the Tories down the line
In Tamworth he wrote it
So now let me note it
Tamworth's the name of a breed of swine

The 'Tamworth Manifesto' of 1834 is seen as laying down the principles on which the 20th century Conservative Party was based.

19th December

Did you know Alzheimer died on this day?
He was really old, that's what they all say
I'm really old too...
And have I asked you?
Did you know Alzheimer died on this day?

On this day in 1915.

20th December

Artur met a jobsworth at the Albert Hall
'I'm Rubinstein, for a piano recital
The people swoon when I play tunes'
'I don't care if you're Charlie Koons
There's no way I'm letting you park here at all'

Rubinstein died on this day in 1982. I think I heard the late
Dennis Norden tell this story.

21st December

I doubt you've heard of the Rochdale Pioneers
They decided each was equal with his peers
And they opened a shop
The first ever co-op
A decision for which we should give three cheers

This day in 1844.

22nd December

About Stonehenge there is a certain doubt
Some say the Druids carried no real clout
But this argument is stronger
That they made the days longer
When they bade the sun 'Stop messing about'

Much is made of the dawn on the summer solstice, but it seems more
plausible that the Druids would have used the temple, which aligns with
sunset on this winter solstice to command the sun to make the days longer again.

23rd December

In Mousehole 'tis Tom Bawcock's Eve
There was no food, so he took leave
Went out in the squall
And caught fish for all:
Stargazy pie? Can you believe...?

This is an annual celebration in the Cornish fishing village,
though the date of the actual event is not given. Stargazy pie
is so called because the heads of the fish stick out of the crust
and look up to the sky.

24th December

Not a creature was stirring, not even a mouse
Except for those children you bred with your spouse
Who won't go to sleep
And then try to creep
Downstairs, to see if Santa has come to their house

25th December

The greatest present to the earth
Must have been Isaac Newton's birth
His laws and relations
Gave sound explanations
Of which back then there was a dearth

Born 1642. Arguably the man who had the greatest influence on
how we live our lives today. (Historians of Science – *Discuss.*)

26th December

Good King Wenceslas looked out
And what he saw made him shout
Coming along the road
Were a couple who glowed
The Curies, without a doubt

Pierre and *Marie* announced their discovery of radium in
1898. They were unaware of its lethal properties.

27th December

In the past it was often all the rage
To take the children to this play on stage
It's about Peter Pan
Who won't become a man
And they tell me the story doesn't age

J M Barrie's play premiered in 1904.

28th December

A train was crossing the river Tay
When gale force winds blew the bridge away
The abominable
William McGonagall
Rhymed 'nine' with 'time' – what else can I say?

The world's worst poet is best remembered for his portrayal of this disaster in 1879.

29th December

Sex Discrimination was banned on this day
Maybe launching Mrs Thatcher on her way
But I get the feeling
She built a glass ceiling
Even today, women don't get equal pay

The Sex Discrimination Act became law on this day in 1975,
paving the way for the Equal Opportunities Commission.

30th December

Richard Rodgers died this day. (You should expect
I mean the composer, and not the architect.)
Who was the better part-
-ner, Hammerstein or Hart?
I'm not sure. Can I have more time to reflect?

Dying in 1979, *Rodgers* arguably had two separate careers. With Lorenz
Hart he wrote songs like *The Lady is a Tramp* and *Ten Cents a Dance*. With Oscar
Hammerstein there was much more *Happy Talking* and *Climb Every Mountain*.

31st December

New Year's Eve is a time to come clean
It's *deja vu* wherever I've been
No matter what I guzzle
I always face this puzzle
What the devil does *auld lang syne* <u>mean</u>?

Well?